THE KEEPERS

THE KEEPERS

An Introduction to the History and
Culture of

THE SAMARITANS

Robert T. Anderson

Terry Giles

First Printing—March 2002

Library of Congress Cataloging-in-Publication Data

Anderson, Robert T., 1928–
    The keepers : an introduction to the history and culture of the
Samaritans / Robert T. Anderson, Terry Giles.
        p. cm.
    Includes bibliographical references and index.
    ISBN 1-56563-519-1 (alk. paper)
    1. Samaritans—History. I. Giles, Terry. II. Title.
DS129 .A57 2002
296.8′17′09—dc21
                                                    2001008158

To my wife, Elizabeth
RTA

In honor of those I love most: Cheryl, Ginny, Will, and Amy
TG

Table of Contents

List of Abbreviations

PRIMARY SOURCES

1 Apol.	Justin Martyr, *Apologia i*
1–2 Kgs	1–2 Kings
1–2 Macc	1–2 Maccabees
1–2 Sam	1–2 Samuel
3 Macc	3 Maccabees
ᶜ*Abod. Zar.*	ᶜ*Abodah Zarah*
ʾ*Abot*	ʾ*Abot*
Acts	Acts
An.	Tertullian, *De anima*
Ant.	Josephus, *Jewish Antiquities*
b.	Babylonian
B. Meṣiᶜa	*Baba Meṣiᶜa*
Bek.	*Bekorot*
Ber.	*Berakot*
Beṣah	*Beṣah (=Yom Ṭob)*
Buildings	Procopius, *On the Buildings*
Demai	*Demai*
Deut	Deuteronomy
Exod	Exodus
Ezra	Ezra
Gen	Genesis
Giṭ.	*Giṭṭin*
Hag	Haggai
Haer.	Irenaeus, *Adversus haereses*
Ḥag.	*Ḥagigah*
Heb	Hebrews
Hos	Hosea
J.W.	Josephus, *Jewish War*
John	John
Josh	Joshua
Ketub.	*Ketubbot*
Luke	Luke
m.	Mishnah

Matt	Matthew
Mic	Micah
Ned.	*Nedarim*
Neh	Nehemiah
Nid.	*Niddah*
ʾOhal.	*ʾOhalot*
Peʾah	*Peʾah*
Pirqe R. El.	*Pirqe Rabbi Eliezer*
Praep. ev.	Eusebius, *Preparatio evangelica*
Ps	Psalm
Qidd.	*Qiddušin*
Roš Haš.	*Roš Haššanah*
Sanh.	*Sanhedrin*
Šeb.	*Šebiʾit*
Šeqal.	*Šeqalim*
Sir	Sirach/Ecclesiasticus
Tanḥ.	*Tanḥuma*
Ter.	*Terumot*
Ṭehar.	*Ṭeharot*
Wis	Wisdom of Solomon
Yebam.	*Yebamot*
Zech	Zechariah

SECONDARY SOURCES

AB	Anchor Bible
ABD	*Anchor Bible Dictionary*
AJBA	*Australian Journal of Biblical Archaeology*
BA	*Biblical Archaeologist*
BAR	*Biblical Archaeology Review*
BASOR	*Bulletin of the American Schools of Oriental Research*
BCH	*Bulletin de correspondance hellénique*
BEATAJ	Beiträge zur Erforschung des Alten Testaments und des antiken Judentums
BJRL	*Bulletin of the John Rylands University Library of Manchester*
BSac	*Bibliotheca sacra*
BZAW	Beihefte zur Zeitschrift für die alttestamentliche Wissenschaft
EAEHL	*Encyclopedia of Archaeological Excavations in the Holy Land*
HTR	*Harvard Theological Review*
ICC	International Critical Commentary
IEJ	*Israel Exploration Journal*
JBL	*Journal of Biblical Literature*
JAOS	*Journal of the American Oriental Society*

NTS	*New Testament Studies*
OTP	*Old Testament Pseudepigrapha.* Edited by J. H. Charlesworth. 2 vols. New York, 1983.
PAAJR	*Proceedings of the American Academy for Jewish Research*
PIASH	*Proceedings of the Israel Academy of Sciences and Humanities*
Qad	*Qadmoniot*
RB	*Revue biblique*
TSK	*Theologische Studien und Kritiken*
ZDPV	*Zeitschrift des deutschen Palästina-Vereins*

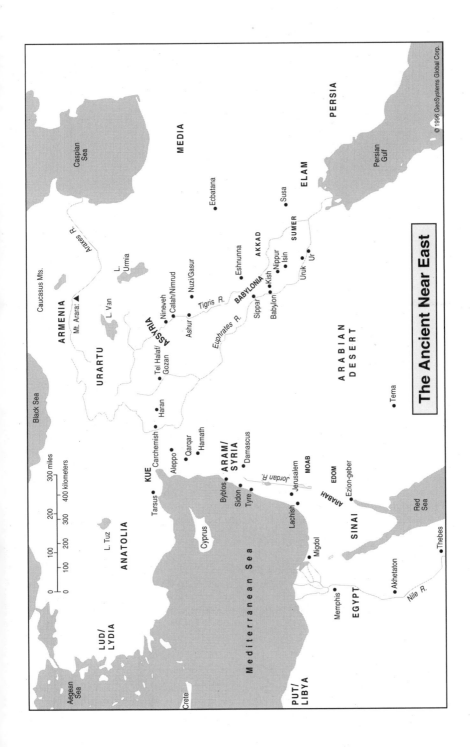

The Ancient Near East

© 1996 GeoSystems Global Corp.

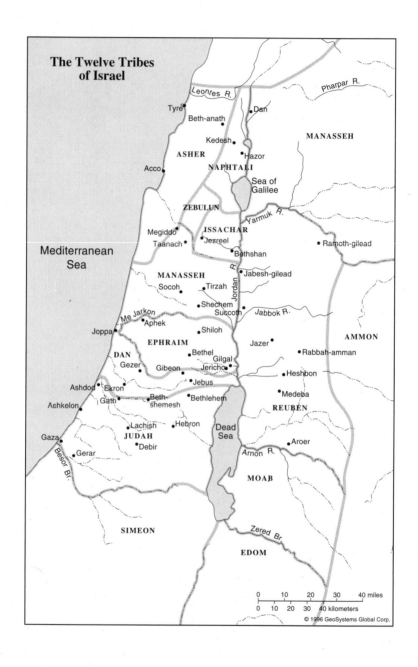

The Twelve Tribes
of Israel

Mediterranean
Sea

MANASSEH

Leontes R.

Pharpar R.

Tyre•
Beth-anath•
•Dan

Kedesh•

ASHER   •Hazor

Acco•   NAPHTALI

Sea of
Galilee

ZEBULUN

Yarmuk R.

Megiddo•   ISSACHAR
Taanach•   •Jezreel   •Ramoth-gilead
•Bethshan

MANASSEH   •Jabesh-gilead
•Socoh   •Tirzah
•Shechem
Succoth   •Jabbok R.

Me Jarkon
Joppa•   •Aphek   •Shiloh

EPHRAIM   Jazer•   AMMON
DAN   •Bethel   •Rabbah-amman
Gezer•   Gilgal
Gibeon•   Jericho•
•Heshbon

Ashdod• •Ekron   •Jebus
Gath•   •Beth-   •Medeba
Ashkelon•   shemesh   •Bethlehem   REUBEN

•Lachish   •Hebron   Dead
Gaza•   JUDAH   Sea
•Gerar   •Debir   •Aroer

Arnon R.

MOAB

Besor Br.

SIMEON   *Zered Br.*

EDOM

0   10   20   30   40 miles
0   10   20   30   40 kilometers

© 1996 GeoSystems Global Corp.

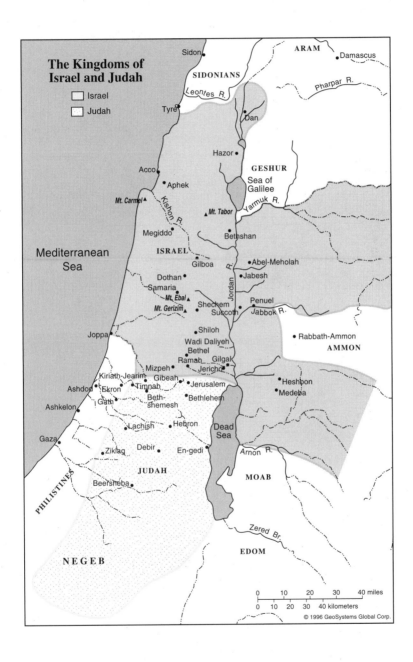

The Kingdoms of
Israel and Judah

☐ Israel
▨ Judah

ARAM
Sidon
Damascus

SIDONIANS
Pharpar R.
Leontes R.
Tyre
Dan

Hazor

Acco
GESHUR
Aphek
Sea of
Galilee
Mt. Carmel
Kishon R.
Mt. Tabor
Yarmuk R.

Megiddo
Bethshan

Mediterranean
Sea
ISRAEL
Gilboa
Abel-Meholah
Dothan
Jabesh
Samaria
Mt. Ebal
Shechem
Penuel
Mt. Gerizim
Succoth
Jabbok R.

Joppa
Shiloh
Wadi Daliyeh
Rabbath-Ammon
Bethel
AMMON
Ramah
Gilgal
Mizpeh
Jericho
Kiriath-Jearim
Gibeah
Ashdod
Ekron
Timnah
Jerusalem
Heshbon
Gath
Beth-
Bethlehem
Medeba
Ashkelon
shemesh

Lachish
Hebron
Dead
Gaza
Sea
Ziklag
Debir
En-gedi
Arnon R.

JUDAH
MOAB
Beersheba

PHILISTINES
Zered Br.

NEGEB
EDOM

0   10   20   30   40 miles
0 10 20 30 40 kilometers
© 1996 GeoSystems Global Corp.

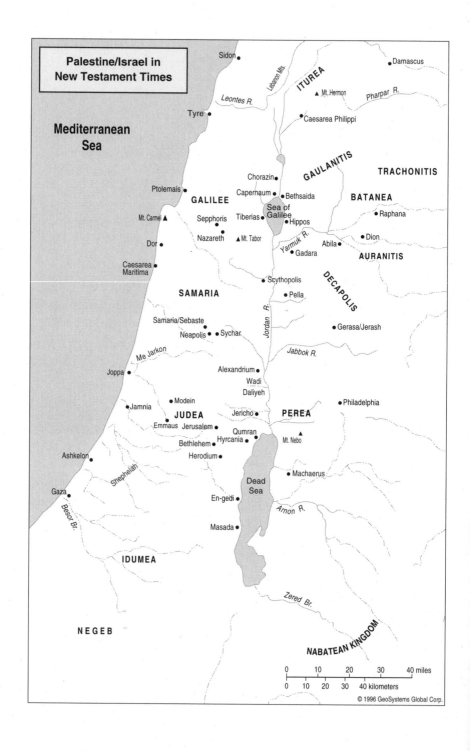

Palestine/Israel in
New Testament Times

Mediterranean
Sea

Sidon

Damascus

ITUREA

Leontes R.

Lebanon Mts.

Mt. Hermon

Pharpar R.

Tyre

Caesarea Philippi

GAULANITIS

TRACHONITIS

Chorazin

Capernaum

Bethsaida

BATANEA

Ptolemais

GALILEE

Sea of
Galilee

Raphana

Mt. Carmel

Sepphoris

Tiberias

Hippos

Nazareth

Mt. Tabor

Dion

Dor

Yarmuk R.

Abila

Gadara

AURANITIS

Caesarea
Maritima

Scythopolis

DECAPOLIS

SAMARIA

Pella

Jordan R.

Samaria/Sebaste

Gerasa/Jerash

Neapolis

Sychar

Me Jarkon

Jabbok R.

Joppa

Alexandrium

Wadi
Daliyeh

Modein

Philadelphia

Jamnia

JUDEA

Jericho

PEREA

Emmaus

Jerusalem

Qumran

Bethlehem

Hyrcania

Mt. Nebo

Ashkelon

Herodium

Shephelah

Machaerus

Gaza

Dead
Sea

Besor Br.

En-gedi

Arnon R.

Masada

IDUMEA

NEGEB

Zered Br.

NABATEAN KINGDOM

0   10   20   30   40 miles
0   10   20   30   40 kilometers

© 1996 GeoSystems Global Corp.

Chapter 1

Introduction

PURPOSE

In 1904, Mr. E. K. Warren, a wealthy American businessman, led a delegation of church school teachers to an international meeting in Jerusalem. When Jacob Ben Aaron Ben Salama,[1] the high priest of the Samaritan community, rose to address one of the sessions, Warren was amazed and enchanted. He had no idea that the Samaritans had survived into the twentieth century. Despite many publications focused on the Samaritans in the intervening years, most Westerners today would share that amazement. The "Good Samaritan" is part of the vocabulary of the West, but the wider context of that allusion and its contemporary referents remain a secret of ethnic and religious history.

This relatively brief work sets out to uncover the history and religion of the Samaritans. It is an ambitious project because the precedents are few, and the subject is often an elusive blip on the screen of history, lost at times in mists of silence or out of focus in historical flights of fancy. The group's origins and much of their history are obscured by contradictory information. They continually present us with intriguing possibilities—a manuscript purported to survive from the time of Moses, stories of miraculous phenomena like a mechanical talking bird, and evidence of a Samaritan migration to medieval Europe. They merged into Judaism at points, counting as a Jewish sect or included in lists of proscribed groups along with Jews and Christians. During times of severe oppression, they dissolved alternatively into Judaism, Christianity, and Islam. During such moments of attrition, they all but disappeared. Waves of dissent fractured them as prevailing heresies like Dositheanism and Gnosticism created serious schisms among them, as well as among Jews and Christians. Both external and internal turmoil has continually threatened their existence, leaving them at times with a population of not much more than a hundred souls.

---

[1] The final chapter will chronicle more about the life and accomplishments of this man.

But survive they did. They survived in part because they were under-girded by a powerful and stable priesthood and in part by sheer chance or, as they would prefer to say, grace. Assuming the theological acumen of the barber of Frederick the Great who saw the survival of the Jews as the greatest evidence for the existence of God, the equally long continuity of the Samaritans likewise can imply an act of divine providence. In part they survived because of their relative political and economic impotence. Their few moments of power invited devastation (at the hands of the first-century B.C.E. Hasmonean leader, John Hyrcanus, and the Byzantine emperor of the sixth century C.E., Justinian, to cite two dramatic incidents that we will describe), but their moments of weakness evoked the "kindness of strangers." For example, the Byzantine emperor Theodosius forbade special taxes upon the impoverished Samaritans; the Christian Germanus helped the Samaritans continue their rite of circumcision after the authorities had forbidden it; the Chief Rabbi of Jerusalem declared to the Ottoman Turks that the Samaritans, like Jews and Christians, were a people of the Book and ought not be persecuted; and the American E. K. Warren built medical and educational facilities for the fragile community at the beginning of the twentieth century.

THE CHAMBERLAIN-WARREN SAMARITAN COLLECTION

Warren facilitated both the survival of the Samaritan community early in the twentieth century and, through the artifacts he protected and preserved, provided valuable sources for understanding the history of this community. Throughout this book you will learn about the Chamberlain-Warren Samaritan collection at Michigan State University, a treasure of Samaritan artifacts that, through a strange sequence of events, became Warren's property and, at his death, was brought to this country. The last chapter will focus more explicitly on his collection. Both the collection and its story deserve comment.

In 1967 an article by J. Strugnell appeared in the *Revue Biblique* describing a series of six Samaritan inscriptions.[2] The first inscription, the author noted, was not available to him except in the form of a casting he had located in Jerusalem. A note dated the casting to the last century. He searched for the original, contacting the American Schools of Oriental Research, the American Institute of Archaeology, the Oriental Institute of the University of Chicago, the University Museum at Philadelphia, and the Kelsey Museum of Archaeology at Ann Arbor. All denied having it. A few months later their de-

---

[2] John Strugnell, "Quelques inscriptions samaritaines," *RB* 74 (1967): 555–80.

nial was substantiated when the missing inscription appeared in a cardboard box in a storage room under the football stadium at Michigan State University.

Many stages of the odyssey of the stone from Jerusalem to East Lansing remain clouded in mystery, but the key link was E. K. Warren, the wealthy churchman from Three Oaks, Michigan, who met the Samaritans during his second visit to Palestine in 1904. He became very involved with the community, giving them financial assistance and acquiring from them a number of manuscripts and other artifacts. In 1950 these and other unrelated items from Warren's collection were given to Michigan State University. The director of the University Museum consulted several universities and museums, sending photographs and descriptions of the marble inscription and the fifteenth-century C.E. Pentateuchs with the explicit suggestion that some other university could make better use of them. Only one scholar expressed any interest at all, and so the materials remained in storage under the stadium until they could be catalogued.

That interval turned out to be eighteen years. In the spring of 1968, Professor Robert T. Anderson of the Department of Religious Studies was asked to evaluate some materials in a storage area that was being reorganized. Three cardboard boxes were marked as part of the Chamberlain-Warren collection and as originating in Palestine. Wrapped neatly inside the first box was the missing inscription Strugnell had described. With some initial guidance from Professor James Purvis of Boston University and from Strugnell himself, a study of the collection began.

The introduction to August von Gall's *Der Hebräische Pentateuch der Samaritaner*[3] provided a clue to the presence of yet another Samaritan treasure at Michigan State. Von Gall referred to a brass scroll case that E. K. Warren had bought. That case was soon located in another storage area of the University Museum. A chance conversation with a librarian led to the discovery of several other rare Samaritan volumes, including a copy of *Memar Marqah*,[4] in the vault of the University Library. The journey of these Samaritan artifacts from Nablus to East Lansing is nothing short of remarkable.

Three years after his initial journey to Palestine, Warren chartered a ship to bring eight hundred delegates to the World Sunday School Association convention in Jerusalem. This was the occasion when Jacob, the high priest of the Samaritan community, addressed the convention, and Warren felt that

---

[3] Adolph von Gall, *Der Hebräische Pentateuch der Samaritaner* (1914–1918; repr., Giessen: Töpelmann, 1966).

[4] John MacDonald, *Memar Marqah: The Teaching of Marqah* (*BZAW* 84; Berlin: Töpelmann, 1963).

it was "the most striking event of the convention." During the next fifteen years, he became increasingly taken with the problems of the Samaritans and determined to help them. He initiated several projects. Some of them, such as the establishment of schools for both boys and girls, were practical. Others were idealistic: he set up a meeting of Samaritans and Jews in Paris with the hope of healing the perpetual rift between the two peoples, and he continued to hope that the Samaritans possessed ancient documents that would verify the gospel accounts about Jesus.

One of his dreams, which eventually determined the arrival of the present collection in Michigan, had an air of practicality, but was never fulfilled. As a means of helping the community to become financially self-sufficient, an American Samaritan Committee was established during the meeting of the World Sunday School Convention at Zurich in 1913 with Warren as chairman and F. S. Goodrich of Albion College (Michigan) as secretary. The most prominent of the other members was the Reverend William E. Barton, an American clergyman who published several articles about the Samaritans and aided in the editing and publishing of works written by the high priest, Jacob. Barton also collected some Samaritan writings that he gave to Boston University.[5]

Although there were efforts to solicit money publicly for the support of the Committee, Warren supplied most of the funds. To raise more money, he had encouraged the publication of photographs of the Abisha scroll (purportedly written by the grandson of Aaron). He expected a reasonable profit to accrue to the Samaritans from the sale of the photos to museums and universities around the world. The photos were taken, but their poor quality, along with the condition of the manuscript and the mistaken judgment of a well-known Old Testament scholar that the manuscript was not authentic, caused them not to sell.

Meanwhile, the Committee was buying such manuscripts and artifacts as it could find to forestall the irreversible dispersal of these treasures out of Palestine. They intended eventually to house the materials in a local museum, assuming that the Samaritans would repurchase their sacred writings and other artifacts and use them to attract a tourist trade that would sustain the community. At the same time, Warren was apparently buying other items, such as a marble inscription and a brass scroll case on his own. Since some of these items remained in Palestine for a long time after their purchase, Warren may have intended that they also be preserved for the day when a museum could be built.

---

[5] James D. Purvis, "Studies on Samaritan Materials in the W. E. Barton Collection in the Boston University Library," in *Proceedings of the Fifth World Congress of Jewish Studies* (Jerusalem: World Union of Jewish Studies, 1972).

In 1919 Warren died, interest in the museum dwindled, the Samaritans had no funds with which to redeem their manuscripts or other artifacts, and, as a result, most of the collection was sent to Three Oaks, Michigan, as part of Warren's estate. Barton wrote in 1921:

> The Committee owns several manuscripts believed to be ancient and deposited in Palestine awaiting its order, and a larger number of recent manuscripts made by the Samaritans. It is agreed that all personal property, excepting photographic plates, belonging to this Committee, shall be forwarded to this country; that the older manuscripts be deposited for the present in the libraries of prominent universities, where they will have care and be available for scholarly study; the recent manuscripts to be placed on sale and the proceeds to be deposited in the treasury of the committee for the ultimate benefit of the Samaritan people.[6]

The collection arrived in this country, but no records explain why none of it reached any university. Rather, it was housed in a museum that Warren had built in Three Oaks to display several collections that his family had brought back from various world travels.

By this time, Warren's dream had evaporated, leaving the Samaritans in unfortunate circumstances. They had neither realized profit from the photographs of the Abisha scroll (described below) nor succeeded in keeping the collection in Palestine. They communicated with the American Samaritan Committee for two or three years trying to secure more money and/or the return of their collection. Barton went to Palestine in 1926 and distributed the assets of the Committee, thus closing this phase in the history of these materials. For the next quarter of a century, the manuscripts remained in the Three Oaks Museum. When the Museum closed a generation later, Fred Warren, E. K. Warren's son, made arrangements, after much consultation with several institutions, to deliver the contents to Michigan State University.

While E. K. Warren's original dream of establishing a museum dedicated to the Samaritan community evaporated with hardly a trace, the fascination captured by these artifacts has not dimmed in the least. Warren gave the Samaritans financial assistance and hope for the future. The Samaritans gave him and, in turn, all of us a broader window into their long history and culture. In the following pages, the story of the Samaritans will be told using, in no small measure, the materials that Warren obtained. These "Keepers of Tradition," the name the Samaritans have given to themselves, refuse to be relegated to the forgetfulness of the past. The following pages recount the most recent chapter in their long and distinguished story.

---

[6] George E. Barton, "The War and the Samaritan Colony," *BSac* 78 (1921): 1–22.

THE SAMARITANS

It is an intriguing story. The Samaritans claim they are the descendants of the northern tribes of Israel (particularly Ephraim and Manasseh) defeated by the Assyrians in 722 B.C.E. (The Jews are the descendants of the southern tribe of Judah.) The Samaritan community is a subculture with a history of well over two thousand years. It preserves vestiges of ancient Hebrew religion. Their practices are rooted in the priestly sacrifices that disappeared in Judaism with the destruction of the temple. The priesthood itself, they claim, is a survival of the priests of Zadok, the only legitimate priesthood since the time of David.[7] The Zadokite genealogy is difficult to trace, and the Samaritan interpretation is historically possible.

The Samaritan community has intersected each of the great civilizations that have shaped Western civilization. Alexander the Great purportedly financed their Holy Place; the Roman governor, Pontius Pilate, lost his position after a complaint from the Samaritan community; and the emperor Justinian practically decimated the community in the sixth century. Samaritan presence is attested in the Hebrew Bible (Christian Old Testament), the Dead Sea Scrolls, and the New Testament. Their unique scriptural text provides evidence for recovering obscure layers of textual development. We do not have the original text of any biblical book, and Samaritan texts help us sort out the order and origin of the several texts that show up at a site like Qumran.

Through Samaritan eyes we can also catch new glimpses of the rise and development of Islam as well as turbulence in the Middle East during the Crusades and the Mongol invasion. Modern textual criticism received tremendous stimulus when Samaritan texts arrived in Europe in the early seventeenth century. Prior to that time, there were two major sources for reconstructing the text of the Old Testament, the Masoretic Text in Hebrew that was stabilized at the end of the first millennium and the Septuagint, or Greek translation, whose earliest copies dated from the fourth century C.E. Roman Catholics supported the Septuagint readings, while Protestants appealed to the Hebrew. The appearance of this third text, the Samaritan, aroused great interest as each side hoped for support from it. This created great interest in understanding the development of the text, as we shall see.

The modern Samaritan community is experiencing a renaissance. It still celebrates the Passover on Mount Gerizim with animal sacrifice, and its members are photographed with their ancient scrolls in front of the syna-

---

[7] 2 Sam 8:17.

gogue at Nablus. Their number is on the increase. They publish their own newsletter and have become increasingly visible. In turn, a growing number of scholars have turned their attention to the Samaritans. In 1985 the Société d'Etudes Samaritaines was founded at a meeting of Samaritan scholars in Paris. That organization has sponsored a series of World Congresses bringing scholars from many nations together to read and discuss papers resulting in several articles and books.[8]

This book consists mainly of a history of the Samaritans, including the archaeological and literary evidence available to trace that history. The history proceeds across several chapters. Two distinctive features of their culture deserve separate chapters: the Samaritan Pentateuch was the artifact that aroused interest in modern times (that is, since the sixteenth century), and the story of its acquisition and use as well as its distinctive features warrant a chapter. A defining characteristic of a Samaritan is religion, which also deserves a chapter. That religion is intentionally conservative and provides new insights on old practices. At the same time, Samaritan religion reveals a long history of adaptation to other faiths, particularly Judaism, Christianity, and Islam. The last chapter describes the pieces of the Chamberlain-Warren collection and their relationships to other existing Samaritan artifacts.

---

[8] A sense of the scope of the studies may be gleaned from papers presented at the conferences, for example, Alan D. Crown and Lucy Davey, eds., *Essays in Honour of G. D. Sixdenier: New Samaritan Studies of the Société d'Etudes Samaritaines* (Sydney: University of Sydney/Mandelbaum Publishing, 1995), and Alan D. Crown, ed., *The Samaritans* (Tübingen: J. C. B. Mohr, 1989).

Chapter 2

Samaritan Origins

INTRODUCTION

The origin and early history of the Samaritan sect are problematic in almost every respect. Trouble begins with the designation of the group as "Samaritans."[1] This term now means a well-defined and self-conscious religious sect employing a version of the Pentateuch called the Samaritan Pentateuch as its sacred text and honoring Mount Gerizim as the proper place of worship. Although many of the members of the group live in Samaria, the term "Samaritan" within this context no longer refers to a geographic region or its inhabitants. This has not always been the case. In some texts, including the Old Testament, the meaning of the term "Samaritan" is not clear. It could refer to residents of Samaria, or to people with a political bent in competition with the political authorities in Jerusalem (rather than to an identifiable religious sect). Consequently, we cannot assume that every mention of "Samaritans" taken from an ancient text refers to the religious sect.

Very likely, the designation "Samaritan" has had a long history of referents and only gradually became identified with a religious sect based in Samaria.[2] In light of this evolving identification, the history of the early Samaritan community will be divided into two sections: (1) the protohistory of the Samaritans, which will include their origins (chapter two) and the journey toward the development of the Samaritan sect (first half of chapter three); and (2) the early history of the Samaritan sect (second half of chapter three). The movement from protohistory to history, that is, the formation of the Samaritan sect, will be identified when three criteria are met: (1) a self-awareness as a religious sect, (2) the use of the Samaritan Pentateuch as the holy text,[3] and (3) the preference for Mount Gerizim as the proper place of

---

[1] Robert T. Anderson, "Samaritans," *ABD* 5:941.

[2] Richard J. Coggins, *Samaritans and Jews: The Origins of Samaritanism Reconsidered* (Atlanta: John Knox, 1975), 7.

[3] See James Purvis, *The Samaritan Pentateuch and the Origin of the Samaritan Pentateuch* (Cambridge: Harvard University Press, 1968), 13–14, for a strong statement correlating the appearance of the Samaritan sect with the Samaritan version of the Pentateuch.

worship.[4] These three criteria will define "Samaritan" as a member of a religious sect and not primarily as a resident of a geographic region or participant in a political ideology.

Using these three proofs to mark the beginning of the religious sect, it is reasonable to identify the Hasmonean period (168–123 B.C.E.) as the stage at which the Samaritan sect clearly emerges on the historical horizon (described in chapter three under the heading "Hellenistic Period"). As it affects the Samaritans, that period begins with the hostilities of the Maccabean revolt and ends with John Hyrcanus's persecution of the Samaritans. It can be demonstrated that the Samaritan sect existed as a self-conscious religious group utilizing the Samaritan Pentateuch and preferring Mount Gerizim as the place for worship in the mid-second century B.C.E. Accordingly, prior to the Maccabean revolt, we can identify and describe the origins and early history of a group of Samaritans, which we will call Proto-Samaritans,[5] and after John Hyrcanus, we can more categorically identify the Samaritan religious sect.

One can object to this approach because it appears to disregard the Samaritans' own claims to ancient origins that reach back to Moses and his immediate successors. This objection can be overcome, however, if we make demonstrable self-consciousness an essential aspect of the sect. Even if the group's roots go far back in the history of ancient Israel, a recognition of that separateness by non-Samaritans only appears in the context of postexilic Judaism. The clear identification of "Samaritan" as a label for a specific religious sect using the Samaritan Pentateuch and preferring Gerizim can be traced with confidence only back to the Hasmonean period.

SAMARITAN VERSION OF ORIGINS

Biblical Background

The Samaritans, who prefer to call themselves Israelites, claim they originate in the time of the judges (eleventh century B.C.E.), when they say the priest and judge Eli established a cult site at Shiloh to rival that at Shechem. Where or how either city became Israelite sites of worship is difficult to state. The earliest accounts are in the books of Joshua and Judges, neither of which

---

[4] That worship on Gerizim alone is not sufficient to determine a separate Jewish sect is evidenced by the temples at Elephantine, Leontopolis, 'Araq-el-Emir, and Qumran. See Coggins, *Samaritans and Jews,* 112, and H. H. Rowley, "Sanballat and the Samaritan Temple," *BJRL* 38 (1955): 166–268. Yet, against this view and arguing that the temple on Gerizim had a strongly divisive effect, see Purvis, *Samaritan Pentateuch,* 10–12.

[5] This designation is suggested already by Jarl Fossum, *The Name of God and the Angel of the Lord* (Tübingen: Mohr, 1985), 42.

is a part of the Samaritan Bible.[6] The Samaritans have a book of Joshua, but it is different from the biblical book, and its sources are later. Joshua, according to the Hebrew Bible, assembled all the tribes of Israel at Shechem for the reading of a new covenant.[7] But earlier "The whole community of Israelites met together at Shiloh and established the Tent of Presence there.[8] Apparently, both sites were important to early Israel. In any event, Shechem eventually became the cultic center for the Samaritans, and Jerusalem, not Shiloh, became the religious center for the Jews. This may have been the chief factor in how each community interpreted the development of the centers of the past, just as Jews denigrated the former sanctuaries at Dan[9] and Bethel.[10]

Samaritan Chronicles

The Samaritans are aware of the Hebrew Scriptures that are not in their own canon and sometimes use them to support their positions and sometimes indirectly dispute them. Still, the major Samaritan sources for periods after the time of Moses are their chronicles.

Abu'l Fath, who in the fourteenth century C.E. wrote the major work of Samaritan history, comments on Samaritan origins as follows:

> A terrible civil war broke out between Eli son of Yafni, of the line of Ithamar, and the sons of Phineas, because Eli son of Yafni resolved to usurp the High Priesthood from the descendants of Phineas. He used to offer sacrifice on the altar of stones. He was 50 years old, endowed with wealth and in charge of the treasury of the children of Israel. . . .
>
> He offered a sacrifice on the altar, but without salt, as if he were inattentive.
>
> When the Great High Priest Ozzi learnt of this, and found that the sacrifice was not accepted, he thoroughly disowned him; and it is (even) said that he rebuked him.
>
> Thereupon he and the group that sympathized with him, rose in revolt and at once he and his followers and his beasts set off for Shiloh.
>
> Thus Israel split into factions.
>
> He sent to their leaders saying to them, "Anyone who would like to see wonderful things, let him come to me." Then he assembled a large group around him in Shiloh, and built a Temple for himself there; he constructed a place like

---

[6] The Samaritans accept only the Pentateuch, the first five biblical books, as Scripture.
[7] Josh 24:1.
[8] Josh 18:1.
[9] Judges 17–18.
[10] 1 Kgs 12: 25–33.

the Temple. He built an altar, omitting no detail—it all corresponded to the original, piece by piece.

Now, he had two sons, Hophni and Phineas, who rounded up young women of attractive appearance and brought them to the Tabernacle which had been built by his father. They let them savor the food of the sacrifices, and had intercourse with them inside the Tabernacle.

At this time the children of Israel became three factions:

A (loyal) faction on Mount Gerizim; a heretical faction that followed false gods; and the faction that followed Eli son of Yafni in Shiloh.[11]

The *Samaritan Chronicle Adler,* or *New Chronicle,* probably composed in the eighteenth century C.E. using earlier chronicles as sources, echoes and embellishes the account of Abu'l Fath:

And so at that time Eli the son of Yafni went and made for himself an ark of gold, wherein he placed the books written in the handwriting of his ancestor, our lord Ithamar. He also made for himself a tent and pitched it at Shiloh, because the children of Israel who were at that time in Shechem and in other cities of Palestine, had driven him from Mount Gerizim, together with those who joined him. There in Shiloh he built an altar and offered sacrifices upon it, and all the men of the tribe of Judah joined him, as well as many men from other tribes. . . .

And the children of Israel in his days were divided into three groups: one did according to the abominations of the Gentiles and served other gods; another followed Eli the son of Yafni, although many of them turned away from him after he had revealed his intentions; and the third remained with the High Priest Uzzi the son of Bukki, in the chosen place, Mount Gerizim Bethel, in the holy city of Shechem.[12]

It is a significant moment for the Samaritans' self-understanding. Historically, it marks the schism between Samaritans and other Hebrews, particularly Jews. It was at Shechem that the Israelites (constituting both the later Jews and Samaritans), under the leadership of Joshua,[13] had reaffirmed their covenant after occupying the land of Canaan, and Shechem was the original holy place of all Israel. From the Samaritan point of view, the move to Shiloh from Shechem was a departure from an orthodoxy that only the Samaritans

---

[11] Abu'l-Fath, *Kitab Al-Tarikh* (trans. Paul Stenhouse; Sydney: Mandelbaum Trust, University of Sydney, 1985), 47–48 (with slight modifications).

[12] *Samaritan Documents Relating to Their History, Religion, and Life* (trans. and ed. John Bowman; Pittsburgh: Pickwick, 1977), 89–90.

[13] Josh 24:1–18 tells the story of Joshua gathering the tribes at Shechem to review their history and establish a covenant with them.

maintained. The Samaritans see in this move misplaced and careless worship as well as immorality. The biblical story in part confirms this picture.[14]

Theologically, this event marked the end of what they looked back upon as the good days, the "Era of Divine Favor," also known as the Age of Grace, Divine Favor, *Ridhwan,* or *Rahuta,* which began with Moses. Now begins the *Fanuta*—the "Era of Divine Disfavor" when God looks away from the people.[15] The latter will last until the coming of the savior, or *Taheb.*

David's transfer of the cultus from Shiloh to Jerusalem only deepened the tension between the orthodox Samaritans and the innovative Jerusalemites. These deviations from the pure Israelite religion began with Eli and Samuel, continued with David and Solomon, and were pursued with vigor by Ezra (the "Accursed" in Samaritan lore) after the Babylonian exile. According to Samaritan tradition, he corrupted the Torah with the addition of "fables, legends, and lies," insisted on a temple in Jerusalem, and falsely claimed that the Samaritans were of Gentile descent.[16] Ezra's guilt is evidenced by his preference for the Assyrian language (Aramaic), while the Samaritans retained the ancient Hebrew language and script. The Samaritans believe themselves to represent the orthodox faith and Judaism to be deviant. This understanding is reflected in their self-designation: *Shomrim* ("keepers" of the Torah). The Samaritans and the Jews agree that the eventual split between the two groups had at its core a division within the priesthood. The Samaritans claim an uninterrupted succession of priests and worship on Mount Gerizim, preserving the ancient traditions of the "House of Joseph."[17]

JEWISH VERSION OF ORIGINS

The Hebrew Bible has often been used as an invaluable and ancient witness to the Samaritan community. Since the bias of the Hebrew Bible differs from the bias of the Samaritan commentaries, it is not surprising that the documents present different versions of the origins of the Samaritans.

The Hebrew Bible actually contains little material pertinent to the Samaritans. As we will see, the several passages often utilized for information about them deal more precisely with "Samarians," that is, with the geographically

---

[14] 1 Sam 2:12–17; 22–25.

[15] For discussion of the eras of divine favor and disfavor, see ch. 9, pp. 139–41.

[16] A reference to 2 Kings 17. See *Chronicle Adler* in Bowman, *Samaritan Documents,* 102–3.

[17] This opinion is not without modern scholarly support. Fossum has written: "I, for one, can see no reason why the Samaritans' own claim regarding their origin can not be based on generally correct memory" (Fossum, *Name of God,* 43).

defined political leadership of the north following the Assyrian resettlements of the eighth and early seventh centuries. Though telling us little about the Samaritan sect, the Hebrew Bible does present a context from which to understand the disapproval that was directed toward any group within Judaism that threatened the privileged position of Jerusalem and the religious organization it represented.

"Accordingly he [the King of Assyria] sent some [authentic Israelite] priests, and they [foreigners brought into Samaria who were subsequently plagued with lions], after being instructed in the ordinances and religion of this God, worshiped Him with great zeal, and were at once freed of the pestilence. These same rites have continued in use to this day among those who are called Chuthaioi (Cuthim) in the Hebrew tongue, and Samaretai (Samaritans) by the Greeks; but they alter their attitude according to circumstance and, when they see the Jews prospering, call them their kinsmen, on the ground that they are descended from Joseph and are related to them through their origin from him, but, when they see the Jews in trouble, they say that they have nothing whatever in common with them nor do these have any claim of friendship or race, and they declare themselves aliens of another race."

Josephus, *Ant.* 9.290–291. Translation: *Josephus* (translated by H. St. John Thackeray et al.; 10 vols.; Loeb Classical Library; Cambridge: Harvard University Press, 1926–1965), 6:153.

Josephus, the first-century Jewish historian who contributed many clues to our quest for the Samaritans, provides an early and clear example of the application of biblical passages to the religious sect. This picture must now be refined and clarified.[18] Flavius Josephus lived from about 38 to 110 C.E. He was of a Jewish priestly family and was in turn an ascetic and a military leader fighting first against Rome and then with it. The change of loyalties earned him a pension and the subsequent leisure to write extensively about Jewish history and the contemporary wars.

2 KINGS 17

Jewish interpretations of the origins of this proto-Samaritan group, beginning with Josephus, initially focus on 2 Kings 17:25–26, which reflects the devastation of the northern kingdom of Israel at the end of the eighth century B.C.E. Two centuries earlier a united Israel had reached its zenith under the leadership of Saul, David, and Solomon. At Solomon's death, a civil war broke out and the former united kingdom split into two kingdoms, Judah in the south with Jerusalem as its capital, and Israel in the north whose

---

[18] *Ant.* 9.288–291; 10.180–185; 11.340–347; 11.4.114–119; 12.257–264; 13.74–79; 13.275–279; 20.118–124.

capital was eventually established in Samaria. The two kingdoms struggled for two centuries, before the emerging superpower Assyria destroyed the northern kingdom.

The biblical account of this defeat, authored or at least edited later in Judah, implies that the later Samaritans descended from peoples deported by the Assyrians from other parts of their vast empire during the middle part of the eighth century B.C.E. Part of the population resettled in Samaria were people from Cuthah, the region surrounding an ancient city of the same name northeast of Babylon, one of the lands conquered by the Assyrians and subjected to this policy of forced migration. Eventually "Cuthean" (or Kuthean) became the Jews' name for the Samaritans and thus a reminder of Jewish contempt for these genetically and, therefore, religiously impure persons. This interpretation of the 2 Kings 17 passage is given its earliest and best expression by Josephus, who viewed the chapter as an anti-Samaritan polemic.[19] It is doubtful, however, that this was the original intention of the biblical author.

The story of 2 Kings 17 asserts that these "Cutheans," deported by the Assyrians, adopted a form of Israelite religion in part as an effort to ward off a plague of lions sent by God to punish them for ignoring the God of the land (vv. 25–26):

> When they first settled there, they did not worship the Lord; therefore the Lord sent lions among them, which killed some of them. So the king of Assyria was told, "The nations that you have carried away and placed in the cities of Samaria do not know the law of the god of the land; therefore he has sent lions among them; they are killing them, because they do not know the law of the god of the land."[20]

These "lion proselytes" were never to be trusted and certainly were not honored with the name "Israelite," because their syncretistic forms of worship recognized a multiplicity of deities "after the manner of the nations among whom they had been carried away" (2 Kgs 17:33). This disparaging characterization of the resettlers in the north can hardly be directed at the Samaritans, for they had not yet formed a group and have never recognized a deity other than the God of Moses. Instead, it is best to understand the critique contained in 2 Kings 17 as applying to any Jews who challenged the centrality of Jerusalem.

The Cutheans are simply the inhabitants of the north, not the Samaritan sect. Sargon's deportation of the indigenous Israelite population probably affected primarily the aristocracy within the city of Samaria. The people

---

[19] *Ant.* 9.288–291.
[20] 2 Kgs 17:25–26.

groups brought into the region replacing the deportees remained a minority. The invectives of the 2 Kings account address this select few and not the general population, about which we know very little, and certainly not a religious sect that had, according to the bulk of evidence, not yet attained a sense of self-awareness.

> The fate of the ten tribes that constituted the northern kingdom of Israel, defeated and deported by the Assyrians in the eighth century B.C.E., has been a subject of often wild speculation. They have been located everywhere from Japan to certain Native Americans. Richard Brothers (1757–1824) claimed that the British were descendants of Ephraim (one of the Northern Tribes). This may have facilitated the immigration of Jews into England in the eighteenth and nineteenth centuries. It subsequently became a basis for anti-Jewish sentiments as some claimed that the British, as descendants of the northern tribes, were the true Israel as opposed to the Jews, who were heirs of the southern tribes. Much of the population of the northern kingdom was probably forcibly assimilated throughout the Assyrian Empire. At least some remnant maintained an identity as Samarians, and some of them may have become proto-Samaritans.

The later part of the account of 2 Kings 17 presents a perspective from the postexilic age[21] written into the mid-eighth-century context (expressed by the "to this day" editorial notation of 2 Kgs 17:34). The final schism between Jews and Samaritans (as 2 Kgs 17:29 calls them) did not occur in one moment of decision in the eighth century but developed over centuries, culminating in a series of fateful events and decisions during the second century B.C.E. Second Kings does seem to reflect authentically an ever-present sense of distrust and competition between the north and south in the eighth century. The account is written from a southern viewpoint and is quick to challenge the north's tendency toward independence. This north-south rivalry goes back at least to the so-called united monarchy, and perhaps to the period of the Judges, and may be rooted in geographical differences. The valleys of the north invited agriculture and the attendant agricultural technology, social structure, and culture. The south was better adapted to animal husbandry. The cultural differences between north and south reflect the historic conflict between the farmer and herdsman (highlighted in the biblical story of Cain

---

[21] This chapter probably contains more than one layer of material. Verse 28 affirms that a northern priest could teach people how to "fear God" and likely comes from an early, favorable source. The comments critical of the north (vv. 34–41) could have been written either by a Deuteronomic editor in the time of Josiah or subsequent postexilic writers of the same school, who wanted to establish Jerusalem and the south as the true heirs of the Israelite tradition. Certain phrases are characteristic of the Deuteronomic reformers of the late seventh century, but the phrase "to this day" would seem to be the last comment from an exilic editor.

and Abel), and it provides the backdrop for the Bible's suspicions of a religious sect claiming to be Israelite but not aligned with Jerusalem. Independence from Jerusalem, an identifying characteristic of Samaritanism, draws unstinting criticism from the authors of the Hebrew Bible.

It is generally recognized that the account in 2 Kings 17 is not objective and unbiased history.[22] The purpose of 2 Kings 17, as well as other passages in the Hebrew Bible (particularly in Chronicles and Ezra), is to highlight the primacy of Jerusalem over any potential rivals. This emphasis dates not to the middle of the eighth century but to the later postexilic age, when changing geopolitical fortunes threatened to undermine the Jewish claim that Jerusalem and its priesthood were central within Judaism. Disparagement of the group that later became the Samaritans, as well as all other rivals from the north and factious parties from the south, was the response to this threatened marginalization.[23]

Other Biblical Accounts

Second Kings 18:34 implicitly condemns the north when it describes how the Rabshakeh, the representative of the Assyrian emperor Sennacherib, chides the Judeans during the reign of the eighth-century king Hezekiah: "Where are the gods of Hamath and Arpad? Where are the gods of Sepharvaim, Hena, and Ivvnah? Have they delivered Samaria out of my hand?" The Rabshakeh's indictment seems confused, for it casts derision on these gods of the north who were imported only after the Assyrian conquest. The Rabshakeh's speech would not have convinced Hezekiah, since these were not the gods from whom the conquered nation of Israel sought help in fighting the Assyrian host. Hezekiah would have agreed with the Rabshakeh that these gods offer no safe haven for Judah in the face of the Assyrian threat.

As many have suggested, the confusion is resolved if we understand this part of the Rabshakeh's speech as an editorial comment expressing the biblical writer's condemnation of the north and the gods that they worshiped after their conquest.[24] The Rabshakeh's speech is a convenient way for the writer to enhance the position of the religious structures of Jerusalem and at the same time ridicule its rivals.

The prophetic books (that is, Isaiah through Malachi) contain indirect evidence that the schism between Jews and Samaritans had not yet taken

---

[22] See, for instance, the excellent presentation of Coggins, *Samaritans and Jews,* 13–19.

[23] See the discussion offered by Ferdinand Dexinger, "Limits of Tolerance in Judaism: The Samaritan Example," in *Aspects of Judaism in the Graeco-Roman Period,* vol. 2 of *Jewish and Christian Self-Definition* (ed. E. P. Sanders; Philadelphia: Fortress, 1981), 92–95.

[24] See James A. Montgomery, *I and II Kings* (ICC; Edinburgh: T&T Clark, 1951), 490.

place by the late sixth and fifth centuries B.C.E. That evidence takes several forms. First, these books are silent regarding the schism. Admittedly, an argument from silence is inconclusive in itself, but it is noteworthy that prophetic texts do not mention a group called Samaritans, even though they condemn many forms of religious observance. Second, prophetic hope for restoration is applied equally to the north and the south, giving no hint of the existence of an irreparable breech such as would be expected if a "Samaritan schism" was a current reality. The prophets do not recognize any condition in the north that would necessarily prevent full restoration.[25]

Jeremiah 41:5 supports the likelihood that no serious religious breach has yet occurred. Following hard on the heels of Gedaliah's assassination, "eighty men arrived from Shechem and Shiloh and Samaria . . . bringing cereal offerings and incense to present at the temple of the LORD." This clearly indicates that representatives from these three cultic sites in the north still respected the temple of Jerusalem. Some, at least, in the regions of the north looked to Jerusalem as an important religious center. Given the preference of the Samaritans for a worship site near Shechem, it seems strange that these eighty men, some from Shechem, sacrifice at Jerusalem if indeed they were Samaritans. The problem disappears, however, if the Samaritan schism had not yet taken place. The exclusivity separating Jerusalem and Gerizim was unknown to the writer of Jeremiah 41.

Ezekiel 37:16–19 anticipates a reunification of all Israel and shows no hesitation about admitting any group from that unified restoration. The two sticks in the hand of the prophet, one representing Judah and the other representing Joseph and Ephraim, are united—"join them together into one stick" that includes the whole house of Israel. This and many other passages in the prophetic literature express a hope for the restoration of the kingdom, both north and south, indicating that the apostasy of the people or any part of it was not perceived as irreparable (Hos 1:10–2:1, "Judah and the people of Israel shall be gathered together"; Zech 10:6–12, "I will strengthen the house of Judah, and I will save the house of Joseph"; Mic 1:5–9, "What is the transgression of Jacob? . . . and what is the high place of Judah?"; Mic 6:16). Ezekiel goes further and presents the north as less culpable than the south, and both may yet experience a return to the Lord. In chapter 23, God reveals to Ezekiel that there are two sisters, Oholah and Oholibah, representing Samaria and Jerusalem, and declares that "Oholibah saw [the sin of Oholah], yet she was more corrupt in her lustings and whorings, which were worse than those of her sister" (v. 11). There is no indication, at least articulated by

---

[25] Thomas Boogaart illuminates this issue in *Reflections on Restoration: A Study of Prophecies in Micah and Isaiah about the Restoration of Northern Israel* (Groningen: Rijksuniveriteit te Groningen, 1981).

Ezekiel and Micah, that any faction within the whole "Israelite" nation was irrevocably removed.

Scholars have identified anti-Samaritan polemics in the writings of Isaiah (particularly chapters 65–66), Haggai (chapter 1), and Zechariah (chapters 1–8). All of these efforts tend to read any opposition to Jerusalem or the religious authorities there as indicative of the presence of Samaritans. If, however, the chief characteristics of the Samaritans are kept in mind, namely, their preference for Gerizim and their loyalty to the Samaritan Pentateuch, then none of the opponents to Jerusalem in these sixth- and fifth-century writings fit the bill. What we can say with certainty is that these passages witness to the divisions occurring within Judaism at this early date.[26] Jerusalem had not yet achieved a universally recognized status, and these texts reflect the competition for that central place of honors.

In sum, then, these two versions of Samaritan origins reveal the bias of each community. The Samaritans view themselves as preservers of an ancient orthodoxy traceable to Moses, and they rely to some extent on the biblical tradition to make this point. The Hebrew Bible, on the other hand, offers little help in understanding Samaritan origins (2 Kings 17 being its prime source), but Jewish interpreters, such as Josephus, expand on this scant and slanted interpretation in order to describe the Samaritans as religiously impure, a result of their syncretistic origins under the Assyrians during the eighth century. Each side of the dispute, of course, can object to the biased claims and interpretations of the other.

---

[26] Coggins, *Samaritans and Jews,* 56–57.

Chapter 3

The Persian and Hellenistic Periods

THE PERSIAN PERIOD

The Samaritan sect begins to bubble to the surface within the roiling caldron reflected in the book of Nehemiah. After the exile, during the Persian period (539–323 B.C.E.), Babylonian Jewry considered itself the preserver of the pure religion of the God of Israel, and one of these Jews, Nehemiah, had the good fortune to become a Persian official. Hearing a report of the deteriorated conditions of the Jewish community that had returned to Jerusalem after the exile, he obtained permission not only to visit the community but to become its governor. Zealous to protect the community's purity, Nehemiah forbade intermarriages with those inhabitants of Palestine who had avoided exile in Babylon:

> In those days also I saw Jews who had married women of Ashdod, Ammon, and Moab; and half of their children spoke the language of Ashdod, and they could not speak the language of Judah, but spoke the language of the various peoples. And I contended with them and cursed them and beat some of them and pulled out their hair; and I made them take an oath in the name of God, saying, "You shall not give your daughters to their sons, or take their daughters for your sons or for yourselves. Did not King Solomon of Israel sin on account of such women: among the many nations there was no king like him, and he was beloved by his God, and God made him king over all Israel; nevertheless, foreign women made even him to sin. Shall we listen to you who do all this great evil and act treacherously against our God by marrying foreign women?"[1]

Nehemiah considered Sanballat, the Persian governor over Samaria, a Gentile. In 432 B.C.E., after Nehemiah had returned to Babylon, one of Sanballat's daughters married a son of the high priest, Joiada. Whether intentionally or not, the marriage would certainly have helped establish cordial relationships between the returned exiles now living in Jerusalem and their distant cousins in Samaria. Nehemiah's return to Jerusalem from Babylon, however, changed this friendly course. He was convinced that the returned

---

[1] Neh 13:23–27.

exilic families should remain pure and issued an ultimatum to the newly married couple, demanding that they leave Jerusalem (13:28). This exclusivity stemming from Jerusalem played a role in the eventual schism between the Judean Jews and the Samaritan group.

The confrontation between Nehemiah and Sanballat[2] is often portrayed as a confrontation between Judaism and Samaritanism, but this depiction, implying that Sanballat had a sectarian Samaritan affiliation, goes beyond the evidence. Sanballat did operate as a political functionary of Samaria. Yet, it is improbable at best that Sanballat, particularly with his pagan name,[3] was a welcome spokesperson for any form of the Samaritan sect. Sanballat allied himself with groups that Samaritans would have avoided (Geshem [2:19] and Tobiah [4:7–8]) and the book of Nehemiah never mentions Shechem or Gerizim, certainly prominent locations that would enter the conversation if Sanballat was a member of the Samaritan sect.

Unlike Nehemiah, Ezra did not criticize the Samaritans. The Samaritans, however, did not return the favor. They may have maligned Ezra because, according to tradition, he established a canon of Hebrew Scripture that extended beyond the Torah (i.e., the Pentateuch, or first five books of the Bible). Second Esdras 14 (an apocryphal book to Jews and Protestants) narrates the tradition that Ezra rewrote the entire Hebrew Bible that had been lost during the exile. On the one hand, that meant that no literature written after Ezra's time could be included in the canon. On the other hand, it did establish the Prophets and Writings (the second and third divisions of the Hebrew Bible) as Scripture, against the judgment of the Samaritans.

Both Samaritans and Jews have credited Nehemiah's contemporary, Ezra, with magnifying the schism between the two communities, and Josephus identifies Ezra as finalizing the split between them. The passage from the Hebrew Bible that focuses on the conflict is Ezra 4, which begins:

> When the adversaries of Judah and Benjamin heard that the returned exiles were building a temple to the Lord, the God of Israel, they approached Zerubbabel and the heads of the families and said to them, "Let us build with you, for we worship your God as you do, and we have been sacrificing to him ever since the days of King Esarhaddon of Assyria who brought us here." But Zerubbabel, Jeshua, and the rest of the heads of the families in Israel said to them, "You shall have no part with us in building a house to our God; but we

---

[2] Nehemiah 4.
[3] Abram Spiro, "Samaritans, Tobiads, and Judahites in Pseudo-Philo," *PAAJR* 20 (1951): 313.

alone will build to the Lord, the God of Israel, as King Cyrus of Persia has commanded us."

Then the people of the land discouraged the people of Judah, and made them afraid to build, and they bribed officials to frustrate their plan throughout the reign of Cyrus, king of Persia, and until the reign of King Darius of Persia.

It is often assumed that the adversaries of Ezra were Samaritans, but a close reading of the passage indicates that Ezra 4 attempts "to uphold the claims of the Jerusalem community and to show how God worked with it, rather than to decry any specific rival group."[4] There is nothing in the Ezra passage that identifies the group receiving the condemnation beyond the broad labels "adversaries of Judah and Benjamin" and "people of the land."[5] It is most likely that the target for criticism is simply the Samarians, that is, the political leaders of Samaria. Even though Josephus interprets this text as a condemnation of the Samaritans,[6] an interpretation that parallels Samaritan understanding of the same events (witness the Samaritan epithet "Ezra the Cursed"),[7] it is unlikely that Ezra 4 identifies the Samaritan sect as the adversaries.

The Chronicler emphasizes throughout that Jerusalem is the center for the worship of God. The Samaritan community, in contrast, champions a different center of worship and reduces Jerusalem to a nonessential. Certainly, the Chronicler would criticize Samaritans for that. But as far as Ezra 4 goes, since the "people of the land" want to help rebuild the temple and to worship there too, it is unlikely that the Samaritan sect is the object of the Chronicler's scornful attention. Nevertheless, this did not stop Josephus from interpreting Ezra 4 as a condemnation of the Samaritans, nor the Samaritans themselves from drawing out of this text the contemptuous title "Ezra the Cursed." Further, they claim that when Ezra rewrote the Scripture, he and Zerubbabel abandoned the old Hebrew characters and made up an alphabet of twenty-seven characters.[8]

If Ezra did not directly oppose Samaritanism, why did he have such a negative reputation within the Samaritan community? Jewish tradition regards Ezra highly, second only to Moses. Samaritan tradition, on the other hand, despises and curses him. The reason for this contradictory reputation must involve those essential conditions that define the schism between Judaism and Samaritanism. The tradition surrounding Ezra equates him with an exclusive

---

[4] Coggins, *Samaritans and Jews,* 66.
[5] Ezra 4:1, 4.
[6] *Ant.* 11.4.114–119.
[7] Abu'l-Fath, *Kitab Al-Tarikh* (trans. Paul Stenhouse), 98.
[8] Abu'l-Fath, *Kitab Al-Tarikh,* 97.

approach to Judaism, an exclusiveness that favored the orthodoxy of Jerusalem against all other points of view. Second, tradition credits Ezra with establishing the canon of the Hebrew Bible. Samaritanism will not recognize the centrality of Jerusalem and will not assent to the same canon in place there. Consequently, Ezra is pivotal in contributing to the self-identity of the Samaritan sect as opposed to the form of Judaism that took shape in Jerusalem.

The Hebrew Bible contains no direct reference to the Samaritans nor any reflection of the Samaritan and Jewish schism. It does, however, provide a general context whereby the differences between the north and the south set the stage for a variety of schisms focused against the political and religious center of Jerusalem.[9] Since schismatic groups are identified and condemned within the Hebrew Bible, other later groups sharing similar censured beliefs could be equally condemned.

Somewhere around 410 B.C.E., Egyptian priests destroyed the temple of the Jews at Elephantine (ancient Yeb, on the Nile River). The Jewish community there had written to Jehohanan, high priest in Jerusalem, seeking his authorization in rebuilding the temple. He considered the temple of Yeb illegal because the Elephantine Jews were not part of the Babylonian exilic Jewry and so not of pure descent. He also would have reservations about the offering of animal sacrifices outside Jerusalem. Failing to receive help from Jerusalem, the Elephantine community wrote to the Samarians in 407 B.C.E., asking for their help and hoping to find a stronger bond with the Samarians than they found with those in Jerusalem. Bagohi, the governor, and Delaiah, the son of Sanballat, responded with permission to rebuild the temple on its original site but prohibited them from offering animal sacrifices.[10]

THE HELLENISTIC PERIOD

Characteristically, the lives and experiences of the Samaritan community during the Hellenistic period (332–31 B.C.E.) remains obscure, with only a few powerful and influential people surfacing in historical documents. Recounting wars and treaties, the intrigue of diplomacy, or the building of monuments and cities can provide a rough outline of the period, but it can never satisfy a quest to understand how the Samaritans felt about themselves and how they got along with their neighbors. Clearly such issues are important and all the more so when we realize that it was in the Hellenistic period

---

[9] Coggins, *Samaritans and Jews*, 80–81.

[10] B. Porten and J. J. Farber translate this correspondence in *The Elephantine Papyri in English* (Leiden and New York: E. J. Brill, 1996).

that the community began to face the inescapable fact that they existed as an unwelcome minority and developed an identity neither Jewish nor Gentile (though viewed at times as both).

Aside from the biblical texts, little is known about the Proto-Samaritan group until Alexander's conquest of Palestine in 332 B.C.E. When Alexander's expedition eastward bogged down during the siege of Tyre, he sent requests for additional personnel and supplies to the various nations in the vicinity. Remaining loyal to the Persians, Jaddua, high priest in Jerusalem, refused to help Alexander. Sanballat III, governor of Samaria, decided to cast his lot with the Macedonian, sensing that it was only a matter of time before he would conquer the Persians. He sent eight thousand troops to aid Alexander and submitted to his rule. In time Sanballat sought Alexander's permission to build a temple in Samaria. This request formalized a building project that was probably complete at the time of the request. Since we only know the story from Josephus, it may be part of a Jewish polemic associating the Samaritans with the despised Greeks. In any case, the act of assistance offered to Alexander during the siege of Tyre coupled with the denial of aid from the Jews in Jerusalem placed the Samarians in a favorable position within the new empire.

Josephus's account of Alexander's activities after arriving in Palestine is suspect and appears to be designed to challenge the trustworthiness of those he labels "Samaritans." Regardless of the degree of accuracy in the details Josephus preserves, it is clear that a significant drama was about to unfold in Palestine. A series of events, however, changed the balance of power among the Jews, the Samaritans, and the Greeks.

The unfortunate chain of miscalculations affecting the fortunes of the Samaritan community began with the appointment of Andromachus as governor over the interior region of Coele-Syria, which included Samaria. During the entire Persian period, one family, the Sanballats, had ruled Samaria. Now the appointment of an outsider as governor set off a violent reaction. In Jerusalem, however, no such response was forthcoming. For the past one hundred years a series of rulers, both Jewish and non-Jewish, had governed the city, so Alexander's appointment was not perceived out of place. Unlike the complacent response of those in Jerusalem, the aristocracy in Samaria reacted violently, burning Andromachus and fleeing from Shechem, eventually seeking refuge in the remote caves of Wadi ed-Daliyeh.

In the spring of 1962 a cache of ancient papyri, jewelry, coins, bullae, pottery, and hundreds of human skeletons were uncovered in several of the many caves lining this steep ravine approximately fourteen kilometers north of ancient Jericho (Tell es-Sultan). These caves were probably the final, unavailing refuge for a group of these aristocrats fleeing the capital city of Samaria.

As the papyri found in one of the caves attest, this group of Samarian aristocrats anticipated resuming their commerce when the military threat subsided, for they carried with them legal documents (property deeds and contracts) required to pick up the pieces of their shattered lives. The skeletal remains in cave one of the group of caves excavated by archaeologists indicate that this plan was misguided. The fugitives clearly underestimated the tenacity of the enemy troops and the ferocity of their vengeance. Evidently, Alexander's soldiers hunted them down, discovered the hideaway, and built a fire at its entrance to suffocate all inside.[11]

The twenty-seven papyri and fragments recovered from the cave can all be dated between 375 and 337 B.C.E. The documents deal primarily with legal matters: the sale of property and slaves, the release of slaves, and the settlement of a legal dispute. While admittedly providing only a partial glimpse into life in fourth-century Samaria, the papyri do reflect political and economic realities of that era. For instance, they mention several governors and prefects, including one Sanballat, perhaps the grandson of the Sanballat in Nehemiah (2:10, 19; 4:1, 7; 6:1, 2, 5, 12, 14; etc.). Slaves were sold for life, in direct violation of Leviticus 25:39–47. And many of the personal names in the papyri are Yahwistic (that is, they include an element of the name Yahweh, the proper name for the God of Israel), perhaps testifying to a popular form of piety within Samaria. Yet, at the same time a number of names contain elements of divine names common among the Moabites, Edomites, Canaanites, and several other population groups, possibly indicating a degree of religious syncretism among at least the Samarian aristocracy. The material found at Wadi ed-Daliyeh cannot be termed Samaritan, based on the criteria established earlier, namely, the presence of a self-aware religious sect worshiping at Gerizim and using the Samaritan Pentateuch. It must rather be called Samarian.[12]

Jaddua, high priest in Jerusalem, took advantage of Alexander's wrath against the Samaritans and met him when he returned from Egypt to deal with the revolt in Samaria. Jaddua pledged to support Alexander, perhaps even revealing the secret location of the Samaritan hideaway. Consequently, this "Samaritan revolt" resulted in the annexation of several Samarian districts to Judea.

Upon the death of Alexander, his kingdom was divided among five of his generals. Seleucus received Syria, including Palestine, though Ptolemy in Egypt also plays a role in the story since Palestine was the site where the gen-

---

[11] This interpretation was first suggested by Frank Cross, "The Discovery of the Samaria Papyri," *BA* 26 (1963): 110–21.

[12] Reinhard Pummer agrees with this assessment in "Samaritan Material Remains and Archaeology," in *The Samaritans* (ed. Alan Crown; Tübingen: Mohr, 1989), 176.

Wilderness of Wadi ed-Daliyeh as it opens onto the Jordan Valley. *Photo by Terry Giles.*

erals' successors, the Ptolemaic and the Seleucid dynasties, fought for control of the region. The Seleucids courted the allegiance of the aristocracy in Jerusalem especially during the time when Simon II (Simon the Just) held the office of high priest. The Seleucids briefly held control over Palestine, suggesting that Simon shrewdly read the political realities of the time. This Seleucid domination, achieved under Antiochus III in 219/218 B.C.E., was short lived, however, as Antiochus met defeat by the Ptolemies in 217 B.C.E. and the region reverted, for a time, back to Ptolemaic rule. As a result of this political intrigue, the districts taken from the Samarians by Alexander were removed from Jewish control and placed back under Samarian domain until at least 145 B.C.E., when John Hyrcanus emerged in Jerusalem as a major political force.

The defeats suffered by Antiochus III were reversed by his successor Antiochus IV. Second Maccabees contains cryptic information about the Samarians during the reign of Antiochus IV. In quelling a rebellion that began with a false rumor of his death, Antiochus IV appointed governors at both Jerusalem and Gerizim,[13] presumably the two centers of the revolt. Later, when Antiochus initiated his cultural cleansings by persecuting the religious Jews of Palestine, he made no distinction between those of Jerusalem

---

[13] 2 Macc 5:22–23.

and those of Mount Gerizim, treating with contempt the sacred precincts at both sites.[14]

Josephus[15] alludes to a letter that a group of Samarians wrote to Antiochus, in which they complain of his treatment as misdirected, for they claim that they are not Jews but Sidonians and should not be subjected to the same treatment as the Jews. While some, with good reason (suspicion of Josephus's bias influencing the text),[16] challenge the authenticity of this letter, Josephus's report can be accepted as valid, and useful information may be gleaned from it. If his information is correct, then it is probable that the authors of the letter were Samarians with a Hellenistic outlook. They wanted to distance themselves from the religious traditions of the past and sought to assert their distinct identity by calling themselves Sidonians. Yet, it is significant that Antiochus could not distinguish between the religious practices of Gerizim and Jerusalem. Certainly not all inhabitants of Samaria belonged either to the Jewish religion or to the developing Samaritan religious sect. Those who were less religiously inclined protested against being identified with the portion of the population that was more so. At the same time, the religious sect at Samaria was not yet distinct from the Judaism of Jerusalem.

Josephus and 2 Maccabees together provide an important clue as to the developing identity of the Samaritan religious sect. At this time the proto-history of the Samaritan sect ends and the history of the sect begins, for it is after the events at the time of Antiochus IV that a self-awareness emerges within the religious community at Shechem.

The evidence for this self-awareness, as one might expect, begins almost imperceptibly but steadily grows during the latter half of the second century B.C.E.[17] The first indication of the distinctness of the Samaritan sect is their failure to participate in the Maccabean revolt (167–164 B.C.E.), which began as a struggle for religious freedom but ended in an effort to purify the land from all cultural and religious dissenters. Despite having a common enemy in the Seleucids, the Samaritans did not take up arms to fight alongside the Maccabees for religious freedom, for they practiced a religion that the Maccabees did not aim to liberate. Later, after the Seleucid expulsion from the land and the gradual Judaization of its inhabitants, John Hyrcanus

[14] 2 Macc 6:2.

[15] Josephus, *Ant.* 12.257–264.

[16] James Montgomery, *The Samaritans, the Earliest Jewish Sect: Their History, Theology, and Literature* (Philadelphia: J. C. Winston, 1907; repr. New York: Ktav, 1968), 78; and Menahem Mor, "The Persian, Hellenistic, and Hasmonean Period," in *The Samaritans* (ed. A. Crown; Tübingen: Mohr, 1989), 14–15.

[17] See Ferdinand Dexinger, "Limits of Tolerance in Judaism: The Samaritan Example," in *Aspects of Judaism in the Graeco-Roman Period*, vol. 2 of *Jewish and Christian Self-Definition* (ed. E. P. Sanders; Philadelphia: Fortress, 1981), 107–8.

(134–104 B.C.E.), the influential high priest in Jerusalem, treated the Samaritans as Gentiles. Even though the Samaritan sect practiced circumcision, their allegiance to Mount Gerizim rather than Jerusalem placed them, in John's opinion, outside the camp of Judaism. The Samaritan refusal to join in the Maccabean revolt indicates their self-recognition as a distinct sect that would not benefit from the religious liberation for which the Maccabees fought. John Hyrcanus's treatment of the Samaritans late in the second century B.C.E. indicates that he too recognized the distinctness of the sect. The acknowledgment of the sect's distinctness by both insiders and outsiders marks the beginning of its singular history in the middle of the second century B.C.E.[18] It is no accident that the recovered manuscripts attesting to the Samaritan sect evidence a separate tradition dating from this time.

Hyrcanus's enemies included the Ptolemies, but the most serious threat came from the Seleucid Antiochus VII, who led a Syrian army against him and besieged Jerusalem, lifting the siege only after Hyrcanus offered him three hundred talents in tribute. Later, however, when Antiochus embarked on a campaign against the Medes, Hyrcanus took opportunity to attack the unprotected cities of Syria on the western end of Antiochus's realm, notably including Samaria, Shechem, and Mount Gerizim. (Although besieged by Hyrcanus, Samaria's final destruction was left to his sons Aristobulus and Antigonus). Hyrcanus's campaign resulted in the destruction of a temple, or whatever sanctuary existed on Mount Gerizim, a sanctuary which had stood on the site for two centuries since its construction during the early years of Alexander the Great.

This destruction may have contributed to a Samaritan diaspora to other parts of the Mediterranean world. In 1979 two Greek inscriptions were discovered on the Greek island of Delos commemorating the substantial contributions by several individuals to the Samaritan community. The sponsors of the inscriptions identify themselves as

"Israelites (in Delos) who make offerings to holy Argarizein."[19]

Neither inscription includes a date, but through paleographic examination P. Bruneau suggests a date of 150–50 B.C.E. for Inscription 1 and 250–175 B.C.E. for Inscription 2.[20]

---

[18] Menahem Mor agrees essentially with this view of the developing self-awareness on the part of the Samaritan sect ("The Persian, Hellenistic, and Hasmonaean Period," in *The Samaritans* [ed. A. Crown; Tübingen: Mohr, 1989], 18).

[19] Pummer, "Samaritan Material Remains and Archaeology," 150. Argarizein = Hebrew for Mount Gerizim.

[20] Philippe Bruneau, "Les Israelites de Delos et la juiverie delienne," *BCH* 106 (1982): 465–504.

The inscriptions are instructive in several respects. First, they provide tangible evidence of the presence of members of the Samaritan sect in the Greek islands. Second, the inscriptions provide a clue to the way in which the group maintained its own identity. Members call themselves Israelites. This favorite self-description implies a degree of solidarity with a broader Israelite group by identifying with the cultural heritage implied in the name "Israelite." Within this large group, the Samaritans viewed themselves as a special subset—those who consider Gerizim the proper place of worship. The Delos Samaritan community demonstrated its dedication and strength of attachment toward the holy mount through votive gifts.

The conquest by Hyrcanus was effective in bringing Samaria under Jewish control for the next half century. Josephus contains no further information about the Samaritans until the Roman occupation under Pompey, leaving us to draw inferences about these intervening years from circumstantial evidence. What can be said with certainty is that Hyrcanus's policies led to alienation between the Jews and at least some of the conquered inhabitants of Samaria. This alienation finds one expression in the growing gulf between Judaism and the Samaritan sect.

The schism between Jew and Samaritan developed over the span of several centuries beginning in the fifth and fourth centuries B.C.E. The relationship between the two groups was fluid, characterized alternately by cooperation and mistrust and suspicion, but when Hyrcanus launched his devastating attack on the Samaritan population, the final split between the two groups became irreversible.

While examples of several text types are found at Qumran, no subsequent unquestionably sectarian text has been found. The "Proto-Samaritan" text type found at Qumran demonstrates a close relationship to the Samaritan Pentateuch, particularly in its practice of making incidents consistent in vocabulary and clarity with any of their parallels. The same words are used in parallel narratives (like the statement of the Ten Commandments), or events are explicitly defined where allusions could be ambiguous. Most scholars believe the Samaritan Pentateuch is derived from the proto-Samaritan text type found at Qumran, but is a later stage in the development of the text type than the Qumran manuscripts.

Literary evidence recovered at Qumran suggests that, although this hostility around 120 B.C.E. clearly defines the date and the protagonists, the Samaritan biblical textual tradition had already developed a history of its own. By the mid-second to mid-first century B.C.E. a distinct Samaritan version of the Pentateuch had already developed, complete with expansionist tendencies imprinting upon the text the sect's viewpoint. Since evidence of the

Proto-Samaritan Pentateuch (particularly the harmonizing or bringing together of similar verses) recovered at Qumran is not accompanied by evidence of a Samaritan version of the rest of the Hebrew canon, there must have been a trend early within the Samaritan community to restrict its canon to the Pentateuch. They demurred from recognizing the prophetic corpus already a part of the sacred text of the Jews. While aware of the other Jewish sacred books, the Samaritans deliberately chose not to recognize them, undoubtedly because of these texts' recognition of the sanctuary in Jerusalem and disparaging attitude toward the north.

All of this means, then, that literary evidence contemporaneous with the formative period of Samaritan history, the Hellenistic era, is scarce. Only a precious few documents from the period mention the Samaritans and offer useful information about them.

> Theodotus in *On the Jews* says that Shechem took its name from Shechem, the son of Hermes, the alleged founder of the city. He says that the city is situated in the land of the Jews in the following manner:
>
> > Thus the land was good and grazed upon by goats and well watered. There was neither a long path for those entering the city from the field nor even leafy woods for the weary. Instead, very close by the city appear two steep mountains, filled with grass and woods. Between the two of them a narrow path is cut. On one side the bustling Shechem appears, a sacred town, built under (the mountain) as a base; there was a smooth wall around the town. . . .
>
> Translation by F. Fallon, in *The Old Testament Pseudepigrapha* (ed. James Charlesworth; 2 vols.; New York: Doubleday, 1985), 2:790.

From the second or first century B.C.E. comes an epic poem written by Theodotus. The identification of this poet eludes modern investigators, who are divided as to whether he was Jewish or Samaritan. His epic poem, the fragments of which were gathered together by Alexander Polyhistor and preserved by Eusebius, retells a story found in the Bible, the rape of Dinah and the sack of Shechem.[21] While some believe that the title assigned by Polyhistor is wrong, asserting that the poem is of Samaritan origin,[22] the majority of scholars agree that Theodotus was a Jewish activist in full support of Hyrcanus's sack of the city of Shechem,[23] and that the poem's title, "On the

---

[21] Gen 33:18–34:31.

[22] Ben-Zion Wacholder, *Eupolemus: A Study of Judeo-Greek Literature* (Cincinnati: Hebrew Union College-Jewish Institute of America, 1974).

[23] Adela Yarbro Collins, "The Epic of Theodotus and the Hellenism of the Hasmoneans," *HTR* 73 (1980): 91–104; F. Fallon, "Theodotus," *OTP* 2:785–89.

Jews," serves as a loose label for a varied collection of material all featuring aspects of Jewish life and tradition.

The poem does fit well with a date before the middle of the second century B.C.E. The epic story contrasts the uncircumcised inhabitants of Shechem (standing in for the Samaritans of the second century B.C.E.) with the circumcised children of Abraham. The children of Abraham visit a righteous vengeance upon the Shechemites, proving both more powerful and more just than their defeated foes of Shechem. It may well be that the hostility that existed between the Israelites and the Samaritans during the reign of Hyrcanus finds expression in this reprise of the conflict between the patriarchs and the inhabitants of ancient Shechem. Minimally, the poem reflects open antagonism between the Jews and Samaritans during the second century B.C.E.

Another germane text is 1 Esdras in the Septuagint (called 3 Esdras in the Vulgate), a continuation of the historiographical traditions of the Hebrew Bible. The book crystallized around a nucleus of material from 2 Chronicles 35 and 36, Ezra, and a small section of Nehemiah.[24] First Esdras 2:1–25 is concerned with the rebuilding of the temple under the auspices of Cyrus and the opposition to the construction on the part of the proto-Samaritans.

Josephus relied upon 1 Esdras for his account of the postexilic period, so the work must have been composed prior to the middle of the first century C.E. As such, it gives additional evidence of the existence of the Samaritan community, but does not clearly demarcate that community as a sectarian, regional, or political unit during the second century B.C.E. The book does not clarify whether the opponents to the reconstruction in Jerusalem are political representatives from Samaria or the Samaritan sect, or both.

Still other texts survive in Eusebius's *Praeparatio evangelica,* where two further quotations deal with the life and travels of Abraham, one of them assigned by Alexander Polyhistor to Eupolemus and the other anonymous. Scholars commonly assign both quotations to Pseudo-Eupolemus. Each could have implications about the Samaritans.

After a brief description of Babylon following the flood, the first quotation describes Abraham as notably wise, particularly as he "sought and obtained the knowledge of astrology and the Chaldean craft."[25] At God's command he traveled to Phoenicia and later to Egypt, in a tale patterned after Genesis 14. In all his travels, Abraham instructs others in his knowledge and understanding.

---

[24] Neh 7:72–8:13.
[25] *Praep. ev.* 9.17.3 (trans. *OTP* 2:880).

Eupolemus: *Praeparatio evangelica*

Eupolemus holds that Abraham was born in the tenth generation in the Babylonian city Camarina, although others state that the city was named Ourie (which mean "city of the Chaldeans") and that Abraham was born in the thirteenth generation. Abraham excelled all in nobility and wisdom; he sought and obtained the knowledge of astrology and the Chaldean craft, and pleased God because he eagerly sought to be reverent. At God's command, he traveled to Phoenicia and dwelt there. He pleased the Phoenician king by teaching the Phoenicians the cycles of the sun and moon, and everything else as well. Later, the Armenians campaigned against the Phoenicians; victorious, the Armenians took captive the nephew of Abraham. Abraham and his servants came to the rescue; they regained control of those who had been taken captive, and they took captives the children and women of the enemy. Ambassadors were sent to Abraham to buy back the prisoners, but he chose not to make profit out of the misery of others: He took what was required to feed his servants, and returned those whom he had captured. *Abraham was treated as a guest by the city in the temple Argarizim, which means "mountain of the Most High."* He received gifts from Melchizedek, its ruler and priest of God.

Translated by R. Doran, in *The Old Testament Pseudepigrapha* (ed. James Charlesworth; 2 vols.; New York: Doubleday, 1985), 2:880.

The second quotation traces the lineage of Abraham back to the giants. One Belos appears as the founder of Babylon, and Abraham once again receives credit for teaching astrology to the Phoenicians and the Egyptians.

The first quotation, in particular, has sometimes been credited not to Eupolemus but to an anonymous Samaritan,[26] for it contains a reference to Salem, as mentioned in Genesis 14, but locates the site at Argarizim, the "Mount of the Most High God" (*Praep. ev.* 9.17.5). This identification of Salem and Shechem need not imply Samaritan authorship, however, for the Septuagint makes the same identification in Gen 33:18. The frequent claim that this fragment's bent toward Hellenism indicates a Samaritan origin is similarly dubious.

Finally, remnants of the work of Cleodemus Malchus survive in Josephus's *Antiquities* (1.239–41) and are cited by Eusebius in *Praep. ev.* 9.20.2–4. Josephus states that he received his material from Alexander Polyhistor. Since Polyhistor dates to about 50 B.C.E., Cleodemus must have written at least by the first half of the first century B.C.E. The fragment that survives deals with the descendants of Abraham through his wife Keturah: Afera and Iafra. In the story, Afera and Heracles fight alongside one another,

---

[26] *Jewish Writings of the Second Temple Period* (ed. Michael E. Stone; Philadelphia: Fortress, 1984), 165.

and from the marriage between a daughter of Afera and Heracles come the founders of Africa.

Freudenthal first made the suggestion that Cleodemus was a Samaritan.[27] The basis of his argument was the syncretistic tendencies evident in the narrative's linking of the descendants of Abraham with Heracles. This evidence, however, is insufficient to demonstrate a connection between Cleodemus and the Samaritan community.

---

[27] Jacob Freudenthal, *Alexander Polyhistor und die von ihm erhaltenen Reste judäischer und samaritanischer Geschichtswerke* (vol. 1/2 of *Hellenistische Studien;* Breslau: Skutsch, 1874–75), 133–34

Chapter 4

The Roman Period

Archaeological data, Josephus, the New Testament, and second-century rabbinic literature open wide windows through which we catch glimpses into Samaritan life during the Roman period. The excavations at Nablus, the Samaritan-populated Neapolis of the Roman-Byzantine era, have revealed a bustling and prosperous city boasting a large theater, hippodrome, and amphitheater. The Samaritans existed as only one portion of the resident population, and it is difficult to know the extent to which they participated in the community functions attested by these great buildings.

Nablus, today a moderately sized city of about 160,000, has a rich history that reaches far back into antiquity. Known to the Egyptian pharaoh Thutmose III, the city is referred to in the Bible as Shechem, renamed Neapolis by the Romans, appears on the mosaic map in Madaba, and was an important site for the Crusaders, Mamluks, and Ottomans.

The current city center is about three kilometers west of the ancient site of Shechem and is nestled in the narrow valley between the slopes of the two dominant mountains in the region, Gerizim and Ebal. As might be expected, the ancient tell of Shechem, Mount Gerizim, its slopes, and the valley underneath, as well as the surrounding region, have all supported extensive archaeological field work that has produced a rich yield of historical and cultural information. As the modern city expands up the slopes of Gerizim and Ebal, new construction and archaeological reclamation both provide unwanted encumbrances to Samaritan access to their holy sites.

About half of the just over six hundred Samaritans living in Israel and Palestine reside in Nablus. Most of the remainder make their homes in Holon, just outside Tel Aviv. The two Samaritan cemeteries, one at the foot of Gerizim and one near its summit, as well as the annual feasts and holy days celebrated on the mountain, insure that Nablus will always be a center of Samaritan life and culture.

JOSEPHUS

The longest and perhaps most ambitious work of Josephus is the *Jewish Antiquities*. Here he traces the history of the Jewish people from the creation to the time of the Roman administration just prior to the war with Rome in 67 C.E. Josephus himself dates his work[1] to the thirteenth year of the reign of Domitian (93–94 C.E.).

Rita Egger argues that most scholars err in portraying Josephus as "anti-Samaritan."[2] The error, she claims, arises because scholars do not distinguish between the Israelite-Samaritans who worshiped at Mount Gerizim and the broader use of the term (preferably Samarians) for a more mixed and widely scattered population. The former group, the Israelite-Samaritans, were integrated equally into the Jewish story. She cites *Jewish Antiquities* 12.7–10, 18.85–89, and *Jewish War* 3.307–315, each of which is characterized in the paragraphs below. Josephus probably did regard the Samaritans as essentially Jewish.[3] He does acknowledge that they are "apostates of the Jewish nation"[4] and that they were sufficiently akin to Judaism that disgruntled Jews felt comfortable seeking asylum with them,[5] but he also qualifies whatever he says positively about the sect.

Many episodes reported by Josephus certainly look anti-Samaritan, including his manner of using the biblical account of the group's putative origins in 2 Kings 17.[6] He also aligns the Samaritans with the tyrannical Greeks, describing their temple as a copy of the Jerusalem temple sanctioned by the Greeks (and willingly dedicated to a Greek deity) and branding their priests malcontent apostates from Jerusalem.[7] It is true, as Shaye Cohen has pointed out, that the two episodes in the *Jewish War* touching on Samaritans are devoid of hostility toward them, but he joins most other scholars in describing the *Jewish Antiquities* as "decidedly anti-Samaritan."[8]

Josephus was clearly dependent upon other literary sources, including a Greek version of the Hebrew Scripture and the works of Cleodemus Malchus, Demetrius, and Eupolemus. In Book 12, Josephus presents his own reworking of the *Epistle of Aristeas*[9] and 1 Maccabees.[10] Josephus supplemented this core material with information from a variety of other sources including official documentation regarding the Samaritans.

---

[1] *Ant.* 20.267–268.

[2] Rita Egger, "Josephus," in *A Companion to Samaritan Studies* (ed. A. D. Crown and R. Pummer; Tübingen: Mohr, 1993), 139.

[3] Louis Feldman and Gohei Hata, eds., *Josephus, Judaism, and Christianity* (Detroit: Wayne State University Press, 1987), 258.

[4] *Ant.* 11.340–342.

[5] *Ant.* 11.340–342.

[6] Feldman and Hata, *Josephus, Judaism, and Christianity*, 259–60.

[7] Feldman and Hata, *Josephus, Judaism, and Christianity*, 259–60.

[8] Shaye J. D. Cohen, *Josephus in Galilee and Rome: His Vita and Development as a Historian* (Leiden: Brill, 1979), 149.

[9] *Ant.* 12.11–118.

[10] *Ant.* 12.241–434.

Josephus's earliest accounts of the Samaritans are the elaboration of the 2 Kings 17 passage and his discussions of Ezra and Nehemiah as already discussed. Book 12 includes an account of a Samaritan general, Apollonius, who attacked Judas Maccabeus and was defeated.[11] According to Josephus, the overall demeanor of the Samaritans is pro-Greek, an interpretation epitomized in Chapter 5, according to which the Samaritans asked to have their temple named Jupiter Hellenius.[12] Second Maccabees gives the story a different twist, claiming that the Greek King, Antiochus, sent an elderly Athenian "to pollute the temple at Jerusalem and dedicate it to Olympian Zeus, and to dedicate the sanctuary on Mount Gerizim to Zeus, God of Hospitality."[13] That account makes the Samaritans no more culpable than the Jews.

Pompey's arrival in the eastern Mediterranean in the mid-first century B.C.E. symbolized a far-reaching social shift that was to redirect the cultural and political development of various Palestinian groups. Among the several political reorganizations that he effected was the transfer of several cities, including Samaria, from Jewish to local control. Samaria became part of the province of Syria.

The governor of Syria, Gabinus, implemented a renovation and new building of sections of the city of Samaria. This building program continued under Herod the Great (40–4 B.C.E.) after he gained control of the city. Herod changed the name of the city to Sebaste, populated it with Gentile immigrants, enlarged and fortified it, and constructed a temple. Not only did Herod assume jurisdiction of the city, but the surrounding region came under his control as well. By the end of the first century B.C.E., most of the Samaritan sect living in Palestine resided in Herod's realm.

Herod treated both Samaritans and Jews harshly, although Josephus claims that one of Herod's wives was a Samaritan.[14] However, Malthace, the woman in question, was probably not part of the Samaritan religious sect but simply a native of Samaria whose Gentile lineage included some earlier immigrants to the area.[15]

Following the death of Herod, the district of Samaria passed to his son Archelaus (4 B.C.E.–6 C.E.) as part of his ethnarchy. A poor ruler, Archelaus was banished by Augustus in 6 C.E. owing to complaints from both Jews and Samaritans about his mismanagement. He had ruled for only ten years. Following these years of misrule, Rome brought the district under the direct rule

---

[11] *Ant.* 12.287–292.

[12] *Ant.* 12.257–264.

[13] 2 Macc 6:2.

[14] *Ant.* 17.19–22.

[15] See James Montgomery, *The Samaritans: Earliest Jewish Sect. Their History, Theology, and Literature* (Philadelphia: 1907; repr., New York: KTAV, 1968), 92–93.

of governors, the first of whom was Coponius, who filled the post from 6 to 9 C.E.

Two stories from the writings of Josephus, even if embellished, betray his contempt for the Samaritan sect. The first describes the defilement of the temple on the eve of Passover sometime during the administration of Coponius. The Samaritans, Josephus notes in passing, spread human bones throughout the temple entrances.[16] The incident serves him as an *apologia* for Jews prohibiting Samaritan entry into the Jerusalem temple.

Mount Gerizim figures several times in narratives that recount conflict between the Samaritans and the Romans. During the tenure of Pontius Pilate (26–36 C.E.) as prefect, a certain "lying Samaritan," as Josephus puts it, led a demonstration on the mount, claiming access to sacred vessels left there by Moses. As Josephus tells the story,[17] Pilate attempted to prevent the large crowd that had gathered from scaling the summit, and the ensuing confusion led to the death or arrest of a number of Samaritans. Pilate, apparently fearing a political conspiracy, perhaps under the guise of a messianic movement, sent troops and had the leaders of the movement executed.[18] This prompted the filing of a formal complaint with Vitellius, governor of Syria, who in turn instructed Pilate to return to Rome to defend his actions before the emperor Tiberius. He was subsequently suspended from his position.

Simon Magus first appears in Acts 8:9–24, where he is a competitor and then a convert to the Christian movement. Given his prominence, his conversion and subsequent closeness to Philip are something of a coup for the early church. But he is shortly condemned for trying to buy the apostles' power to bestow the Holy Spirit by the laying on of hands. Simon seems to repent, but no more is heard of him in the New Testament. When the early church fathers talk about Simon, they align him with Gnosticism and point out, correctly, that his claim to be someone great is a Samaritan concept. Neither Gnosticism nor Samaritanism (or the buying of church office, "simony") were considered worthy of Christianity by the orthodox church fathers.

The leader of this demonstration on Gerizim may have been the infamous Simon Magus, perhaps, as a number of ancient writers thought, the Simon of Acts 8.[19] No direct evidence supports this ancient suggestion, but

---

[16] *Ant.* 18.29–30.
[17] *Ant.* 85–89.
[18] Against the suggestion that this was a messianic movement, see Bruce Hall, "From John Hyrcanus to Baba Rabbah," in *The Samaritans* (ed. A. D. Crown; Tübingen: Mohr, 1989), 39.
[19] For example, Irenaeus, *Haer.* 1.23; Tertullian, *An.* 34.2.

there is ample reason to conclude that Simon was active in Samaria. According to Acts 10 and 11, the Simon of Acts 8 was not a Gentile, but there is also no evidence to suggest that he was a member of the Samaritan sect. Some later traditions suggest that he was a Samaritan, but this appears unlikely, if Irenaeus is correct in presenting him as referring to himself as "first God."[20]

Assuming that Josephus is correct in attributing religious motives to the leaders of the movement, it is almost certain that Pilate's victims were from the Samaritan sect. This event struck a devastating blow to the integrity of the sect. Not only did a significant portion of the leadership die, but the event even further marginalized the sect within this part of the Roman realm.

The other event that reflects the anti-Samaritan bias of Josephus occurred during the tenure of Cumanus as governor in Judea, when the Samaritans killed a pilgrim from Galilee on his way to Jerusalem.[21] Antonius Felix was procurator of Judea, so the incident must have occurred between 52 and 59 C.E. Several Jews and Samaritans died during prolonged communal unrest.

In *Jewish War* 3.7, Josephus describes a later siege on Mount Gerizim in which 11,600 Samaritans, "depending on their weakness," die at the hands of Roman soldiers.[22] Crossan suggests this may have been a passive resistance protest.[23] A Samaritan inscription presumably describes the same episode:[24]

והא בעעת רביע היה מובא תראואן ארור שמו
אל ארץ פלשתים מפני פסבסבאן מלך רומה ועמו צבאות רבים
וייצר אתנו חדש ימים על הר גריזים עד תם הנשם
ואין מים לשתות וקטל מכת ארב כעשר אלף מאנשו חנ͏י͏[ל]ן

Behold, in the time of the rainy season Trajan, cursed be his name, came into the land of Palestine from Vespasian, king of Rome, with his great army; and he blockaded us a full month on Mount Gerizim until the end of the rain and there was no water to drink and he killed among us with the sword about 10,000 soldiers.

This reference to Vespasian is obviously anachronistic, assigning him his later imperial title; he was then governor of Syria.[25] Although the inscription has the number of Samaritan casualties at about ten percent less and the length of the siege as a month longer, there is little doubt that Josephus and

---

[20] Irenaeus, *Haer.* 1.23. See also Justin Martyr, *1 Apol.* 26.
[21] *Ant.* 20.118–124; *J.W.* 2.3–8.
[22] *J.W.* 3.307–315.
[23] John D. Crossan, *The Historical Jesus* (San Francisco: Harper, 1992), 161.
[24] Strugnell, "Quelques inscriptions samaritaines," 562.
[25] Described by Strugnell, "Quelques inscriptions samaritaines," 561–68.

the inscription recount the same event. Spin control is hard to establish. Josephus may have exaggerated the speed of the massacre, or later Samaritans may have extended the time period to a month so as to defend their ancestors' warrior skills.

NEW TESTAMENT

As the New Testament story pans across the first-century Palestinian landscape, Samaritans often figure in the picture, sometimes inconspicuously in the background, sometimes at the very center of the drama. The gospel writers, particularly Luke and John, express ambivalent attitudes about them. Moreover, Stephen's speech in Acts 7, with its curious Samaritan context and numerous hints, also asks for attention. An extensive literature exists on the Samaritans and the New Testament.[26]

Explicit New Testament data on the Samaritan sect is sparse and ambiguous, concentrating mostly on their affect on Christianity. Some Samaritans were probably an audience of the New Testament writings and early participants in Christianity. Galilee was the point of origin for Christianity, and the Samaritans were geographical neighbors. Not only Mark and John but also Q are probably products of Galilee. C. H. H. Scobie posits another hypothetical source—sharing the same provenance as Q—that was the Samaritan source used by Luke.[27] This would mean that Samaritans were involved in the Christian movement from the beginning. Certainly their low economic and social status would predispose them to accept the Christian message.

Willi Marxsen, one advocate of the Galilean provenance of Mark (primarily on the basis of the "return to Galilee motif" [16:7] and other editorial activity), includes Pella in his definition of Galilee. Others include the cities of the Decapolis and Tyre and Sidon as part of the region. The gospel of John equates Galileans and Samaritans, also reflecting much knowledge of the Samaritans. The antipathy to Jerusalem, Jewry, and the temple, reservations about a Davidic Messiah, the focus on "Israel" rather than "Jews," and apocalyptic anticipation—all of these themes in the canonical gospels could have been inspired by Samaritan Christians or the desire to appeal to Samaritan Christians. The Johannine school, in turn, may have provided the middle ground for the move from early Palestinian Jewish Christianity, centered in

---

[26] For a listing see Robert T. Anderson, "Samaritan Studies and Early Christianity," in *New Samaritan Studies* (ed. Alan Crown and Lucy Davey; Sydney: Mandelbaum, University of Sydney, 1995), 121–31.

[27] Charles H. H. Scobie, "The Origins and Development of Samaritan Christianity," *NTS* 19 (1973): 397.

Galilee, to Hellenistic Jewish Christianity, centered in Jerusalem. Tensions and parallels among Samaritans, Christians, and Jews in the New Testament can illuminate our understanding of each.

"In the days of Jonathan, the messiah was persecuted, and the governor killed him in the days of Tiberius the king. He was crucified, he and the 12 persons of his company, in Jerusalem. All of them were placed in a sarcophagus. I (Abu'l Fath) have found in an old Hebrew chronicle that two persons (only) were crucified with him."

Abu'l Fath, *The Kitab al-Tarikh* (trans. and ed. Paul Stenhouse; Sydney: Mandelbaum Trust, University of Sydney, 1985), 147.

Synoptic Gospels

Only Mark among the gospel writers fails to mention the Samaritans at all, but even the second gospel may reflect concessions to the sect. According to Matthew, the initial instruction Jesus gave in sending off the twelve disciples was, "Go nowhere among the Gentiles, and enter no town of the Samaritans, but go rather to the lost sheep of the house of Israel" (Matt 10:5–6). Similar negative feelings toward the Samaritans, but a more irenic attitude on Jesus' part, appear in a cryptic episode in Luke 9:51–56. Messengers enter a Samaritan village to make preparations for Jesus as he travels to Jerusalem. The Samaritans are unwilling to accommodate the party because they are headed for Jerusalem. The disciples are ready to burn the village, but Jesus rebukes them. The conciliatory stance of Jesus, and implicitly by the church retelling the story, is a significant aspect of the story. Two other episodes in Luke speak more sympathetically of the group: the story of the Good Samaritan (Luke 10:25–37) and the account of a Samaritan, the only one of ten healed lepers, who returned to thank Jesus for the healing. Hostility toward the Samaritans has disappeared by the time of the narrative of Acts 8:4–25, which describes them as the next target of Christian mission after Jerusalem and Judea. Philip succeeds in converting Samaritans to Christianity.

Gospel of John

In contrast to Acts 8, John 4:39 attributes the initial Samaritan conversions to Jesus. It is possible that the circumstances by which the first Samaritans entered Christianity are no longer accessible to us and that of these accounts, one or both is ahistorical. It is also possible that there is ambiguity regarding the identification of the inhabitants of the city of Samaria. The story in John certainly deals with members of the Samaritan sect. The woman in conversation with Jesus is aware of the distinctions between Jew and Samaritan (4:9), especially the preference of Gerizim over Jerusalem as the proper place of worship (4:20). Finally, John 4:39 implies that "Samaritan" does not equal the inhabitants of the region, for the Samaritans were not the only inhabitants of the city in which the woman lived. Rather, "Samaritan" in John means a member of the sect.

Another interesting reference to Samaritans appears in John 8:48, where the label is an insult for Jesus equivalent to demonic possession. Jesus replies only that he is not possessed by a demon!

Acts

Acts 8:5–6 indicates that the first conversions to Christianity from among the Samaritans were a result of the preaching of Philip. This could be an alternative narrative to John's description of Jesus' missioning among the group. It could also be that Jesus' experience was with sectarian Samaritans, while Acts describes early missionary work among geographical Samaritans where the Philip-Stephen group seems to have been influential. The last may have been a northern, even Galilean, Jewish sectarian group that shared with the Samaritans an aversion to the Jerusalem temple and its cult. Jewish "Christianity" could therefore appeal to Samaritans in a way that Judean "Jewishness" could not.

Stephen's speech in Acts 7 has been a major preoccupation of Samaritan studies in relation to the New Testament.[28] Stephen's use of a Samaritan type text of the Hebrew Bible, his emphasis on Samaritan heroes, and his modification of the Hebrew text in favor of the sect's concerns mark him as one who either is of Samaritan background or has a history of appealing to such an audience. In either case, Samaritans played a strong role in early Christianity.

SECOND-CENTURY RABBINIC LITERATURE

A variety of rabbinic literature makes reference to the Samaritans.

This is the general rule: In any matter where they [the Samaritans] are under suspicion they are not to be believed. (*m. Nid.* 7:5)

---

[28] An early discussion of this possibility is a summary of the ideas of Abram Spiro in Johannes Munck, *The Acts of the Apostles* (AB 31; Garden City, N.Y.: Doubleday, 1967), 285–300. It was subsequently treated by Coggins, *Samaritans and Jews;* Simeon Lowy, *The Principles of Samaritan Biblical Exegesis* (Leiden: Brill, 1977); W. Harold Mare, "Acts 7: Jewish or Samaritan in Character?" *WTJ* 34 (1971): 1–21; Earl Richards, "Acts 7: An Investigation of the Samaritan Evidence," *CBQ* 39 (1977): 190–208; and Dennis D. Sylva, "The Meaning and Function of Acts 7:46–50," *JBL* 106 (1987): 261–75.

Some feel that the influence of the Samaritans on the New Testament deserves more attention. A few have gone to the other extreme, practically making the New Testament a Samaritan book. According to this later group of interpreters, there is a basic New
Testament Samaritan cast that includes Jesus himself. Jesus did not deny that he was a Samaritan in John 8:48, and according to Heinrich Hammer cited the Samaritan, rather than
the Jewish Pentateuch. The first Christian martyr, Stephen, also cites the Samaritan Pentateuch in his speech in Acts 7 and is the leader of the "Seven," a Hellenistic group, in Acts 6.
Philip, the second of the "Seven," preached in Samaria. In addition some scholars have pre-
sumed Samaritan implications behind every reference to "Israel," "Hebrew," any Samaritan
idiom, or any pentateuchal hero. The epitome of this position is Hammer's *Traktat vom
Samaritanermessias: Studien zur Frage der Existenz und Abstammung Jesu* (Bonn: Carl Georgi,
1913). Abram Spiro, a professor of Near Eastern Studies at Wayne State University, re-
stated many of these themes in the 1960s and '70s.

Samaritan tradition, on the other hand, perhaps wanting to assure Christians that they
played no role in the crucifixion of Jesus, claimed during the Renaissance that, "Now Jesus
the Nazarene did not consult the community of the Samaritan Israelites at any time in his
life. He did not stand in their way nor did they stand in his. They did not impose upon him,
nor he on them in any way. He was, however, the subject of vengeance on the part of his
own people. . . ."

John MacDonald and A. J. B Higgins, "The Beginnings of Christianity according to the Samaritans," *NTS* 18 (1972): 55–80.

This "general rule" deals with matters of ritual cleanness and illustrates the
degree of separation existing at times between the rabbinic authorities and
the Samaritan community. The Samaritans are not accorded the status of Israelite but neither are they considered Gentile (*m. Ber.* 7:1, *m. Demai* 5:9). A
Samaritan may offer a benediction that can be affirmed with an "Amen," but
not until the whole benediction has been heard (*m. Ber.* 8:8). This qualifica-
tion presumably insured the integrity of the benediction voiced by one of
questionable status. But this negative pronouncement was not the only available understanding, for contradictory opinions also existed, as illustrated by
the statement of R. Simon b. Gamaliel:

> Every command the Samaritans keep, they are more scrupulous in observing
> than Israel. (quoted in *b. Ber.* 47b)

The talmudic sources provide valuable information regarding the relationship between the Jewish and Samaritan communities between the second and the sixth centuries C.E.[29] A comparison of the Mishnah (completed

---

[29] The editing of the Talmud under the direction of Christian censors effected on
occasion a change in terminology regarding the Samaritans which can now be somewhat

second century C.E.) with the commentary on the Mishnah found in the Babylonian Talmud makes clear that the final separation of the Jewish and the Samaritan communities took place over time and that the Samaritan sect occasioned considerable debate within rabbinic circles.[30] A man who became a proselyte for the sake of a woman or a woman who became a proselyte for the sake of a man met the same skepticism otherwise reserved for the "lion-proselytes," i.e., the Samaritans (*b. Yebam.* 24b).

While often incensed over the manner in which they observe matters of ritual cleanliness (*m. Nid.* 4:1; *b. Git.* 7b; 10a, 10b), the talmudic sources rarely criticize the ethical behavior of the Samaritans, notably never accusing them of the typical Gentile sins of bestiality or incest.[31] Moreover, at least hypothetically, Samaritans were welcome to seek the advice of rabbinic authorities in settling disputes (*b. B. Meṣiᶜa* 69a).

Distinctions between the two groups extend to the acceptability of offerings (*m. Bek.* 7:1), the observance of holy days (*b. Roš Haš.* 22b; *b. Besah* 4b), and the validity of legal testimony received from a Samaritan (*b. Git.* 1:5). And this separation was destined to continue. The rabbis forbade marriages between Israelites and Samaritans:

> All who are forbidden to enter the congregation may intermarry among themselves. But R. Judah forbids it. R. Eliezer says: "They that are of assured stock may intermarry with others who are of assured stock, but they who are of assured stock may not intermarry with them that are of doubtful stock, nor they who are of doubtful stock with others who are of doubtful stock. These are of doubtful stock: the silenced ones, the foundling, and the Samaritan." (*m. Qidd.* 4:3)[32]

The "silenced ones" are those who know the identity of their mother but not their father. The "foundling" knows the identity of neither parent. The grouping here indicates that at this point the rabbis still considered the Samaritans Jews but did not accord them benefits of full membership into the community. Marriage conventions insured segregation.

This placement of the Samaritans somewhere between Gentiles and Israelites is well illustrated in *m. Demai* 6:1 in a directive about a rented field:

---

misleading. The favorite rabbinic term for Samaritan was "Cuthean" or "Kuthim," a disparaging term taken from 2 Kgs 17:24. This term was easily understood as a substitute for *goyim*, or Gentile, with a much broader designation than originally intended. The relevant Mishnaic passages are: *Ber.* 7:1; 8:8; *Demai* 3:4; 5:9; 6:1; 7:4; *Šeb.* 8:10; *Ter.* 3:9; *Šeqal.* 1:5; *Roš Haš.* 2:2; *Ketub.* 3:1; *Ned.* 3:10; *Git.* 1:5; *Qidd.* 4:3; *ᵓOhal.* 17:3; *Ṭehar. (Tohoroth)* 5:8; *Nid.* 4:1, 2; 7:3, 4, 5.

[30] See Montgomery, *Samaritans,* 166–67.

[31] See *b. ᶜAbod. Zar.* 15b.

[32] The English translation of this and subsequent citations of the Mishnah are from Herbert Danby, *The Mishnah* (Oxford: Oxford University Press, 1933).

If a man rented a field from an Israelite, or from a Gentile, or from a Cuthean (i.e., Samaritan) . . .

This liminal condition allowed a range of relationships between the two communities.[33] At times the tension was high:

> They also told him that R. Eliezer said: "He who eats bread [baked] by Samaritans is like one who eats the flesh of a pig." (*m. Šeb.* 8:10)

Some concluded the Samaritans were unalterably unclean,[34] while at other times the relationship between the two groups appears more cordial. Commenting on proper commercial dealings, the Talmud speaks favorably regarding the character of the Cutheans, implying that "they are not to be suspected" (*ᶜAbod. Zar.* 15b). *Moʾed Qatan* 12a suggests a pragmatic approach applicable to the observance of ritual regulations. During peaceful times, the two communities could respect each other's religious practices; not so during times of stress.

In addition to the differences in ritual observances separating the two groups, the Samaritans distinguished themselves from the Jews by using a different sacred text, avoiding devotion to Jerusalem, and to a lesser degree adhering to certain beliefs in variance from so-called mainline Judaism. Examples of the way in which these three characteristics appear in the mishnaic and talmudic literature are discussed below.

On occasion, rabbinic literature groups the Samaritans doctrinally with the Sadducees:

> The daughters of the Sadducees, so long as they are in the habit of walking in the paths of their fathers, are to be regarded as Samaritan women. If they left those paths to walk in the paths of Israel, they are to be regarded as Israelitish women. (*m. Nid.* 4:2)[35]

This text has to do with ritual cleanness and the perceived deficiencies on the part of both the Sadducees and the Samaritans. A hint of a further doctrinal distinction is found in *m. Sanhedrin* 10:1:

> All Israelites have a share in the world to come, for it is written, "Thy people also shall all be righteous; they shall inherit the land for ever, the branch of my planting, the work of my hands that I may be glorified." And these are they that have no share in the world to come: he that says there is no resurrection of

---

[33] See also *m. Ketub.* 3:1; *m. ʾOhal.* 17:3; and *m. Ter.* 3:9.

[34] *M. Nid.* 4.1 concludes that Samaritan women are unclean, as are those who cohabit with them. The only way, according to this pronouncement, to remedy the uncleanness is to eliminate the community.

[35] See also *m. Ṭehar.* 5:8.

the dead prescribed in the Law, and [he that says] that the Law is not from Heaven, and an Epicurean.

The Sadducees and the Samaritans come under the rubric of those who "say there is no resurrection of the dead prescribed in the Law."

Certainly, one of the more contentious differences between Jews and Samaritans concerns the proper place of worship. That this issue was in the foreground for both Jew and Samaritan is evidenced by the following from *m. Nedarim* 3:10:

> If a man vowed [to have no benefit] from "them that keep Sabbath," he is forbidden to have benefit from Israelites and Samaritans; if from "them that eat garlic," he is forbidden to have benefit from Israelites and from Samaritans; but if "from them that go up to Jerusalem," he is forbidden [to have benefit] from Israelites, but not from Samaritans.

Here, both groups keep the Sabbath and follow ritual dietary practices, but the devotion directed to Jerusalem distinguishes one group from the other.

Likewise, some authorities (R. Judah in particular) determined that a Cuthean (the nomenclature for Samaritans derived from 2 Kgs 17:24) should not be allowed to perform a circumcision because he does it in the name of Mount Gerizim (*b. ʿAbod. Zar.* 26b–27a). The prohibition is owing to the Samaritan's scrupulous insistence that the rite be performed in the name of Gerizim, that is, "attaching a person to the community of Gerizim."[36]

Finally, the biblical text was a mark of distinction between the rabbinic authorities and the Samaritans. The text is marked off in two ways. First, the very script used was an indicator of difference between the two groups.

M. Sanhedrin 2:4, while commenting on the duties and privileges of the king, quotes Deuteronomy 17:19:

> He must write out a scroll of the Law for himself. . . . It shall be with him and he shall read therein all the days of his life.

While commenting on this Mishnah, *b. Sanhedrin* 21b–22a explains:

> Mar Zutra or, as some say, Mar 'Ukba said: "Originally the Torah was given to Israel in Hebrew characters and in the sacred [Hebrew] language; later, in the times of Ezra, the Torah was given in Assyrian script and Aramaic language. [Finally], they selected for Israel the Assyrian script and Hebrew language, leaving the Hebrew characters and Aramaic language for the *hedyototh*." Who are meant by the *hedyototh*—R. Ḥisda answers: "the Cutheans (Samaritans).'"

A second and more fundamental difference in the two groups' Bibles lay in their contents. *B. Soṭah* 33b contains this hypothetical dialogue:

---

[36] Montgomery, *Samaritans*, 170.

R. Eleazar son of R. Jose said: "In this connection I proved the Samaritan Scriptures to be false. I said to them, 'You have falsified your Torah but you gained nothing thereby. You declare that "the terebinths of Moreh" means Shechem. We have learned this by an inference from analogy; but how have you learned it'!"

This confrontation centers around the expansionist tendencies within the Samaritan Pentateuch when compared to the Masoretic Text. The phrase "terebinths of Moreh" ends the verse in Deuteronomy 11:30 in the Masoretic Text, while the Samaritan Pentateuch adds a clarifying explanation, "over against Shechem," in order to locate the site. R. Eleazar's point was that even though the identification is correct, the Samaritans confirmed that conclusion by adjusting their sacred text and so falsifying it.

The final split between the Jewish and Samaritan communities finds bitter expression in the religious literature. The Samaritans are called "those senseless folk that live in Shechem" (Sir 50:26) while the Samaritans favored Jerusalem with the title "cursed house." Rabbinic texts demand the excommunication of the Samaritan community in this fashion:

> Let no Israelite eat of one morsel of anything that is a Samaritan's; let no Samaritan become a proselyte, and allow them not to have part in the resurrection of the dead.[37]

At the end of the fourth Seder in the Babylonian Talmud is a series of tractates called the "Seven Jerusalemite Booklets."[38] The sixth in the series is a collection of directives, *Masseket Kutim,* bearing on relations with the Samaritans. This collection is culled from talmudic and other sources, sometimes reapplying originally anti-Gentile texts to the Samaritans. This reappropriation of texts provides a glimpse into the process that led to the change of status that Jews granted to the Samaritan community. Consider the opening line of the *Masseket:*

> The usages of the Samaritans are in part like those of the Gentiles, in part like those of Israel, but mostly like Israel.

Any reparation between the two communities is only an unlikely possibility. The *Masseket* ends:

> When shall we take them back? When they renounce Mount Gerizim, and confess Jerusalem and the resurrection of the dead. From this time forth he that robs a Samaritan shall be as he who robs an Israelite.

---

[37] *Tanḥ. Vayesheb* 2; *Pirqe R. El.* 38. As quoted by Montgomery, *Samaritans,* 195.
[38] See Montgomery, *Samaritans,* 196–203, for a translation and notes.

Since the Samaritans will, in all likelihood, never renounce Mount Gerizim, there seems little danger of inadvertently robbing an Israelite when reaching into the pocket of a Samaritan.

Josephus and the rabbinic midrashim imply the existence of two leaders within the Samaritan movement: Sabbaeus and Theodosius (Dositheus). These two may have been the nuclei of two sects within the Samaritan group in the first century C.E.[39] The Dosithean sect apparently emerged in the wake of the destruction of the Samaritan sanctuary on Mount Gerizim by John Hyrcanus in the late second century B.C.E. According to Abu'l Fath, the Dositheans split into eight groups. They were more open to synagogue worship, differed on the dating and means of celebrating the feasts, and permitted the pronunciation of the name of God. These all seem various ways of confronting the orthodox priests. The schism continued until the period of the Renaissance, when a reconciliation among the various sects occurred. The origin and number of these sects remains problematic. Some identify Sabbaeus, Dositheus, and Dusis as the same person, and there is controversy whether he or they date from pre-Christian or Christian times.[40] Certainly a schism among the Samaritans between a more priestly-centered and a more lay-centered group began at the turn of the eras and continued until at least the fourteenth century C.E.

Each of these sources—Josephus, the New Testament gospels, and the rabbinic literature—agree that in the first century C.E. tensions were rife between the Jews and the Samaritan sect. The key dispute over the proper place of worship no doubt spilled over into civil, community, and economic matters. The tension felt between the two communities is reflected in a section from the Mishnah: *Roš Hašanah* 96. Although not completed until around 200 C.E., this section of the Mishnah may reflect earlier tensions between the two communities. In a practice that predates the destruction of the temple in 70 C.E., the beginning of the observance of a holy day was marked by the lighting of signal fires starting in Jerusalem and spreading to outlying areas so that even those far away would know when the observance began. The instructions in the Mishnah insist on confirmation from a messenger, because the Samaritans were in the practice of lighting fires at wrong times in order to mislead those living far from Jerusalem.

Certainly, the Babylonian Talmud preserves evidence for a complex set of attitudes by the sages toward the Samaritans. These animosities grew dur-

---

[39] Stanley Isser, *The Dositheans: A Samaritan Sect in Late Antiquity* (Leiden: Brill, 1976), 162–63. Abu'l Fath identifies eight Dosithean sects, although he thinks that one Dusis rather than anyone named Dothesius is their founder (see Stenhouse, *The Kitab al Tarikh of Abu'l Fath*, 223–30).

[40] A discussion of these issues is found in Jarl Fossum, "Sects and Movements," in *The Samaritans* (ed. Alan Crown; Tübingen: Mohr, 1989), 293–389.

ing the Second Jewish Revolt (132–135 C.E.) when foreign invasion plunged Palestine into political chaos.

Hadrian, who reigned in Rome from 117 to 138 C.E., determined to unite his empire upon Hellenistic values and ideals. This goal required the elimination of cultural differences. In Palestine, this meant the establishment of Aelia Capitolina and a ban on circumcision. He inaugurated these policies during his visit to the land in 129 C.E. Much earlier, Vespasian had established in Samaria a Hellenistic city, Neapolis (formerly Shechem; 72–73 C.E.), so that fifty years later the Hellenistic bent of Hadrian could be understood, by some at least, as a natural extension of old policies. For the Samaritan sect, however, the ban on circumcision was as troublesome as it was to the Jews, and they too rebelled against the emperor and his policies. As Eusebius records, Gerizim and Jerusalem were both destroyed as Hadrian eliminated those who resisted his planned cultural assimilation.[41]

The *Samaritan Chronicle* notes that the violence inflicted by Hadrian included random burning, looting, and killing of sages and judges as well as the helpless and defenseless.[42] As in the dangerous time of Alexander the Great, the caves at Wadi ed-Daliyeh again became the refuge of some trying to escape the Roman sword. The archaeological evidence remaining in the caves suggests that the caves' safety was illusory, just as it had been three centuries earlier, and many of the Samaritan refugees died there.

The failure of the rebellion against Hadrian in Samaria was owing to two factors. First, a substantial military presence in Neapolis prior to Hadrian's visit in 129 C.E. limited the opportunity for insurrection. Second, since the policies of Hadrian offended the Samaritan religious sect but not the general population of the area, the limited scope of the rebellion gives evidence of the relative weakness of the Samaritan sect in the early second century. Long Hellenistic influence in the region meant that only a minority of Samaria's inhabitants identified themselves as part of the sect. As evidenced by the violence against Gerizim and the caves at Wadi ed-Daliyeh, this minority was committed but not numerous enough to effect widespread protest during the Second Jewish Revolt.

---

[41] Stewart Perowne, *Hadrian* (London: Hodder and Stoughton, 1960), 166.
[42] Stenhouse, *The Kitab al Tarikh of Abu'l Fath,* 160–62.

Chapter 5

The Byzantine Period

Under Christian Byzantine rule, the Samaritans moved from economic and religious prosperity and widely established habitation in Palestine to near extinction. Amid oppression, however, the Samaritans reached a peak of theological and organizational sophistication and increased in number. Still, it is not likely that the oppression is overstated. Since the Romans had crushed Jewish power, and embattled Byzantine leaders were too busy fighting among themselves to spend much energy on the Samaritans, some expansion of Samaritan freedom and power occurred. Yet, the legal evidence strongly argues that the sect was even more vigorously and systematically repressed than the Jews. A Samaritan religious renaissance took place in the face of these adverse conditions. Persecution solidified their religion; their religion made them more visible, and visibility attracted further oppression.

PROSPERITY

Artifacts from the early Byzantine period suggest that the Samaritans experienced a cultural and religious revival beginning in the third century. Aside from specifically religious artifacts, Samaritan material culture differs little from that of the Jews or Gentiles living in the region. For this reason, it is wise to remain cautious when attempting to identify archaeological findings as "Samaritan." Still, archaeology does have much to offer about the early history of the Samaritan community.

Qedumim, an archaeological site located about ten kilometers west of Nablus, is situated in an area that literary sources report to have been dotted with Samaritan settlements during the Roman-Byzantine era. Jewish sources refer to this area as "a strip of Samaritans," suggesting that it was inhabited predominantly by the sect.[1] The site was excavated in the late 1970s and early 1980s.[2]

Qedumim appears to contain two distinct periods of occupation. The first period, from the third to the fifth centuries C.E., suggests a prosperous

---

[1] B. Hag. 25a. Quoted by Pummer, "Samaritan Material Remains and Archaeology," 162.

[2] Yitzhak Magen, "Qedumim," in vol. 1 of Excavations and Surveys in Israel (112 vols. to date; Jerusalem: Israel Department of Antiquities, 1982), 96–100.

population with well-built houses of hewn stone. This period ended in destruction in the fifth or sixth century. The rebuilt settlement was much less prosperous with buildings of unhewn stone arranged without any corporate city plan.

Perhaps the most interesting finds recovered at Qedumim are the three oil presses and six *miqva'ot*, three connected to the presses and three not associated with other permanent structures. The *miqva'ot* are caverns hewn into the bedrock measuring approximately three by four meters each. Plaster lines them entirely, including the ceiling and steps descending down into the pool. The bottom step is higher than the others. Presumably, when the *miqva'ot* were in use, this step was submerged in water and perhaps also served as a bench. The three *miqva'ot* associated with the presses suggest that the oil processed there was used in religious rituals and that ritual purity was maintained in its manufacture. The existence of these *miqva'ot* dating from the first century C.E. testifies to the fact that the Jews and the Samaritans shared some ritual practices.

Excavations at Qedumim showing *miqva'ot*. Photo by Terry Giles.

Several surviving Samaritan inscriptions probably date to this period. Since the material culture of the Samaritans differed little, if at all, from that of their neighbors, the identification of an inscription as Samaritan is based upon its script and at times by the use of quotations from favorite passages in the Samaritan Pentateuch.

The inscriptions appear on artifacts ranging from stone lintels, lamps, and metal amulets to silk Torah mantles and tomb inscriptions. Most of the inscriptions are short, and some of the artifacts bearing them have no certain archaeological provenance, thus limiting their value. Often, the only way to date the inscription on an artifact is by comparing the shape and style of the script with that appearing on another inscription of a known date. The resulting comparison can be misleading, for the Samaritan engraver often used archaic script or mixed different script types on one inscription rather than using the common contemporary form of letters.

Many of the inscriptions are quotations from the Samaritan Pentateuch and so are valuable witnesses to its transmission. Favorite texts commemorated in the inscriptions include Exodus 12:3, 11, 18; Numbers 10:35; and Deuteronomy 33:26. The following discussion of Samaritan inscriptions includes only a representative selection of the many available.[3]

The First Emmaus Inscription (so called because there are at least three Samaritan inscriptions said to have been found at Emmaus) was discovered in 1881. The inscription is etched into an Ionic marble capital. The inscription is bilingual; on one side is the Hebrew phrase

ברוך שמו לעולם

Blessed is his name forever

On the other side of the capital and appearing in Greek is the phrase

ΕΙΣ ΘΕΟΣ

One God

The size of the capital on which the inscription appears suggests that it decorated a public building, probably a synagogue. The inscription is generally dated to the first century C.E., although some suggest it better fits the first century B.C.E.

The Second Emmaus Inscription was discovered by Lagrange in 1890.[4] The text of the inscription includes portions from Exodus 15, a text favored by Samaritan engravers.

יהוה גבור במלחמה יהוה
שמו יהוה נחיתו
בא ברוך יהוה
אין כאל ישרון

---

[3] A full list of Samaritan inscriptions appears in Reinhard Pummer, "Inscriptions," in *The Samaritans* (ed. Alan Crown; Tübingen: Mohr, 1989), 190–94.

[4] Marie Joseph Lagrange, "Inscription samaritaine d'Amwas," *RB* 2 (1893): 114.

YAHWEH is mighty in battle, YAHWEH
is his name; YAHWEH, you have led him.
Come you blessed of YAHWEH;
There is none like the God of Jeshurun

The Third Emmaus Inscription was recovered by Lagrange in 1896. Although poorly preserved, the text can be read as follows:

ופסח יהוה על הפתח

ולא יתן המשחית לבא

YAHWEH will pass over the door,
And he will not permit the Destroyer to enter

Housed in the library at Michigan State University in East Lansing is a marble stone, presumably used as a lintel, which is now fractured on the left side. On the extreme left edge of the first line of text a portion of a letter appears suggesting that following the ב beginning the third word of the line either a ה or a ח was written next. Upon the remaining piece of stone is written a Samaritan inscription taken from Exodus 15:3, 11.[5] Reproduced in modern script, the text reads:

יהוה גיבור ב

מי כמוך באי

נדרי בקדש נור

YAHWEH is mighty in . . .
Who is like you among the [gods]
Glorious in holiness, Mighty . . .

The inscription shows significant and expected variations from the Masoretic Text, as well as from von Gall's edited version of the Samaritan Pentateuch and the Second Emmaus Inscription. As a close comparison with other renditions of these verses shows, the marble inscription shares characteristics of what later became divergent manuscript families. The inscription on the marble stone provides evidence of a degree of unity in the textual tradition that later became varied in the manuscripts consulted by von Gall.[6]

In addition to evidencing characteristics that point to the unity of the various traditions recording this text from Exodus, the marble inscription

---

[5] The stone is trapezoidal in shape and measures 31.0 x 12.2 x 5.0 cm.

[6] The manuscript groupings that seem to be suggested by the lintel are von Gall's G1, N, P and A, B, C.

The Chamberlain-Warren Samaritan Marble Inscription (CW 2472), one of four inscriptions found at Emmaus, a village twenty miles from Jerusalem on the road to Joppa. *Courtesy of Special Collections, Michigan State University Libraries.*

also hints at a stage of textual development not otherwise recorded. Moreover, it is worth noticing that no manuscript or fragment listed by von Gall, nor any other Samaritan inscription, reads the letter sequence בה following גיבור or its alternative גבור in line one (Exod 15:3) besides this marble inscription. Assuming that the mystery letter (either ה or ח) is intentional and not a craftsman's mistake, the identity and function of this letter must be deduced without the benefit of direct comparative textual evidence. Since Exodus 15:3 was a favorite passage of the Samaritans, often appearing on inscriptional artifacts, it seems odd that this inscription records the text differently from all the rest (see, for instance, the Second Emmaus Inscription above).

In all likelihood, the letter fractured at the left side of the stone was ה. The word intended in line one is no doubt בהמלחמה.[7] The ה following the ב probably functioned as a definite article.[8]

---

[7] Strugnell, "Quelques inscriptions samaritaines," 555–80.

[8] Terry Giles, "The Chamberlain-Warren Samaritan Inscription CW2472," *JBL* 114 (1995): 111–16, with comments on the grammatical issues. The definite article, normally elided after a prepositional prefix, was commonly retained in Israelite Hebrew as recently demonstrated by Gary Rendsburg, *Linguistic Evidence for the Northern Origin of Selected Psalms* (Atlanta: Scholars Press, 1990).

If the definite article is indeed present, line one of the inscription can be read as follows: "The Lord is mighty in the war . . ." This reading emphasizes an event that is archetypal in nature and offers an explanation for the lifting of the phrase from Exodus 15:3 and its attachment to 15:11. Rather than referring only to the defeat of Pharaoh, the lintel, by inserting the definite article, reminds the faithful of God's help and presence in the battle yet to come. The text shifts from a statement of God's help in the past to a statement of hope for God's help in the future.

The text preserved in stone reflects the values of those responsible for the engraving and presents a piece of information about the theology of the Samaritan community at the time of the lintel's inscription. If the reading offered above is correct, it may suggest that the faithful were aware of their tenuous position as a segregated community.

The shape of the letters of the inscription on the lintel is consistent with a date in the sixth century (or perhaps a bit earlier).[9] Perhaps the text's hoped-for victory grew out of the ruthless oppression of the Samaritan community under Justinian. The hostility experienced by the Samaritan sect during that emperor's ruthless reign could easily have expressed itself in hope for God's protection, and this the marble's presence over a doorway offered to all the faithful who passed through.

The inscription found at Beit al-Ma, about one kilometer west of Nablus, is on a stone about one meter long, probably a lintel in a synagogue or other public building. It consists of the Decalogue in an abridged form consistent with that on other inscriptions. The inscription almost certainly predates Justinian, and it may date as early as the third century.[10] The Beit al-Ma inscription is not unique, for a number of other Samaritan Decalogue inscriptions also originated prior to Justinian's reign (Shechem Decalogue, Leeds Fragment, and the Sychar Decalogue).[11]

Several amulets have been recovered from this early period that bear inscriptions written in the so-called Samaritan script. Many of the amulets contain stereotypical phrases from the Samaritan Pentateuch. These artifacts are relevant to the history of the community.

However, one must take care in using these artifacts as historical evidence. The amulets have been, and still are, manufactured for sale or trade to non-Samaritans. Consequently, the owner of the amulet need not have been a member of the community.[12]

---

[9] Giles, "Chamberlain-Warren Samaritan Inscription," 115–16.

[10] See W. R. Taylor, "A New Samaritan Inscription," *BASOR* 81 (1941): 1–6.

[11] John Bowman and Shemaryahu Talmon, "Samaritan Decalogue Inscriptions," *BJRL* 33 (1951): 211–36.

[12] Reinhard Pummer, "Samaritan Amulets from the Roman-Byzantine Period," *RB* 94 (1987): 251–63.

Proceeding cautiously, we note that the amulets, sixteen of which from the Roman-Byzantine era have been catalogued by R. Pummer, are inscribed with quotations from the Pentateuch or in some cases short pious phrases in Greek.[13] Among the pentateuchal quotations, a phrase lifted from Exodus 15:3 recurs with relative frequency:[14]

יהוה גיבור

YAHWEH is mighty

Also appearing often are phrases taken from Deuteronomy 6:4 and 33:26. At least one amulet bears a depiction of a rider and horse, while on another a lion appears.

J. Kaplan has identified two amulets that contain the phrase

ואת שר צבאו

and the commander of his army

Kaplan argues that this phrase is a reference to Baba Raba, the Samaritan revolutionary now thought to date from the third century C.E., who was banished to Constantinople (see below).[15] Kaplan contends that the amulets with this kind of inscription were popular with his sympathizers, and so provide a witness to the extent of his political and religious influence.[16] Various scholars have argued that these inscriptions reflect a revolutionary political spirit, but this remains difficult to prove.[17]

In general, the inscriptions and the figures appearing on the amulets all emphasize the power of the deity or the devotion and trust properly given to God. Since several of the amulets have come from non-Samaritan sites, it is unwise to attempt to suggest a common use of all of the artifacts.[18] Like jewelry containing religious motifs today, these amulets may have served a range

---

[13] Pummer, "Samaritan Amulets."

[14] Jacob Kaplan is of the opinion that this phrase was a "regular opening formula" inscribed upon the amulets at least by the fourth century C.E. Jacob Kaplan, "Two Samaritan Amulets," *IEJ* 17 (1967): 160.

[15] Kaplan, "Two Samaritan Amulets," 196–98.

[16] The same phrase appears on an amulet published by Jean Margain, "Une nouvelle amulette samaritaine portent le texte d'Exode 38.8," *Syria* 59 (1982): 117–20. While Margain finds Kaplan's interpretation of the phrase plausible, he does not deny that the phrase may simply be an abbreviated quotation of Exod 38:8.

[17] Montgomery, *Samaritans,* 115.

[18] Hamburger asserts that these amulets are evidence of a "special amulet magic," assuming a common and single purpose for the amulets. This seems unwarranted, and the conclusion that Samaritans were employed by other religious groups to inscribe phrases on the amulets and so "enhance their magical power" goes beyond the evidence available. See Anit Hamburger, "A Greco-Samaritan Amulet," *IEJ* 9 (1959): 43–45.

of functions, from valued jewelry with a pleasing design, to a cherished expression of a religious or political ideal, to a wish for, or symbol of, the deity's
protection and care.

Baba Raba

The initial stage in the Samaritan religious revival was the product of
one of the greatest and most colorful figures of Samaritan history, Baba Raba.
The chronology of that moment is problematic. One tradition says that
Germanus, bishop of Nablus, who was present at the Council of Nicea in
325, provided protection at the illegal circumcision of Baba Raba. But the
authenticity of the tradition is uncertain, and current consensus is moving
toward a third- rather than fourth-century dating, following the chronicle of
Abu'l Fath, which dates the life of Baba Raba from 222 to 254. He was the el-
dest son of the high priest Nathaniel, a purported associate of Amram, the father of Marqe, the significant Samaritan theologian discussed below. He
lived only thirty-two years.

Baba Raba was a leader with obvious charismatic qualities whom Abu'l
Fath describes as "a powerfully-built man, of awe-inspiring appearance; a
man of zeal and holy spirituality."[19] His persona, coupled with his vision and
organizational skills, revived the depressed and powerless community. In
terms echoing the terror of Hebrews 11:32–40, Abu'l Fath describes the de-
spair of the Samaritan community. Then, parallel to the earlier part of Hebrews 11, he places in the mouth of Baba Raba the inspiring parade of
witnesses to faith—Levi, Simeon, and Pinhas—reaching into the past to provide a model for the future. Such listings of model leaders of the past *(enco-
mia)* were popular among Jews (Sir 44; 1 Macc 2:51; 4 Macc 18; Ps 105;
Wis 10; Acts 7; and Heb 11) and even more popular among Samaritans, particularly in the prayer books and at least a dozen in the *Memar Marqe*. Some
believe the author of Hebrews may have intentionally appealed to the Samaritans with such devices. Echoes of other parts of Hebrews appear in Samaritan
works.[20]

He revived the council of sages *(Hukama)*, appointing three priests and
four laypersons (thus showing strong support to laity) to interpret Samaritan
law, administer justice, offer advice, and tour the synagogues looking for
signs of negligence. The hereditary role of councillor was highly respected
and provided an indigenous guiding group that made the Samaritans less dependent on Judaism. The hymn writer Amram Dare, father of Marqe, served
on the original *Hukama*. Samaritanism, no longer dependent upon the high

---

[19] Stenhouse, *The Kitab al Tarikh of Abu'l Fath*, 173.
[20] John MacDonald, *The Theology of the Samaritans* (London: SCM, 1964), 402.

priesthood at Nablus, could widen its diaspora, since authority had moved to the more mobile council of seven and the laity.

The Dosithean controversy, which had originated in the late first century as a lay-oriented movement, still divided the Samaritan community at a time when it needed unity to face external threats. Baba Raba showed his genius in his success as an ameliorator. The constitution of the council of sages reflects a compromise between orthodoxy and Dositheanism. However, not all accepted compromise. The Sabuai, members of a Dosithean sect, were active in the villages in the time of Baba Raba, though Abu'l Fath reports that they did not heed his reform.

Other actions of Baba Raba seem to mark, in part, a compromise among the feuding sects. He replaced some priests with laypersons who were authorized to perform all the priestly tasks except carrying the Holy Book. He inspired new liturgy and theology that would focus all groups on a common present rather than a divided past. In association with Baba Raba, Amram Dare created new liturgy, assembling less controversial liturgical works from the past and composing new works acceptable to all Samaritan groups.

Baba Raba also inspired an extensive building program. He built eight synagogues and divided Palestine into twelve districts, a Samaritan version of the visionary ideal of the prophets that all Israel, both northern and southern tribes, would one day be reunited and revived. It is a vision that neither Jews nor Samaritans in their narrow parochialism often espoused, but by noticing that the wide settlement of Samaritans across Palestine could symbolize their occupation of the old tribal lands, Baba Raba caught sight of the possibility of a "Pan-Israelite" community.

The thirteenth-century chronicler Abu'l Fath sensed that some of the stories associated with Baba Raba were legendary. For example, he reports the silencing of the mechanical bird that warned the Romans of the approach of any Samaritan to Mount Gerizim, just to register that he has heard the tale. The story reports that Levi, a nephew of Baba Raba, went to Constantinople, converted to Christianity, and became a bishop. Later, he returned to Nablus and went up on Mount Gerizim. The bird in question calls out, "Hebrew, Hebrew," alerting the reader of the story, but not the bishop's entourage, that Levi is still a Samaritan in his heart. Levi convinces his "fellow" Christians that since there is no Hebrew on the mount, the bird is useless and worthy of destruction. The Christians have thus been outwitted in their attempt to exclude Samaritans from the mountain. The story may reflect Byzantine concerns that Samaritan conversion was not always sincere, or Samaritans' real efforts to gain personal benefits like jobs and inheritances as well as to infiltrate the power structure. As a "convert" within the church, Levi successfully undermined the Christians and gave Samaritans access to the mount.

The name Baba Raba literally means a "great gate," and many have pointed out that similar titles have been characteristic of Middle Eastern religious leaders for millennia.[21] The title was popular among Muslims and not unknown among Christians and Jews. The play on "great gate" may have given rise to the odyssey of significant doors (great gates) early associated with Baba Raba. During the reign of Arcadius (395–408), a period of relative calm for the members of the sect, they bribed the emperor to gain a set of bronzed doors that Hadrian had looted from the temple in Jerusalem for use in the temple to Zeus that he had built on Mount Gerizim. (Where the doors had been between the destruction of the temple in 70 C.E. and Hadrian two generations later is not clear.) The Samaritans then proceeded to use them to adorn their synagogue at Nablus.[22] This was Kneshet Hapnina ("The Pearl"), a fairly large synagogue. Later, the doors were reused (or do we have simply a variant tradition?) in another synagogue, Chien Jakub ("Mourning for Jacob"), which still stands but has been converted into a mosque. Finally, according to the story, the Turks confiscated them and took them to Istanbul, where Ben Zvi claims they remain to this day. Whether history or Samaritan polemic, the story probably does reflect Byzantine toleration of Samaritans at least until ca. 400.

In spite of such peaceful coexistence with the state, other stories portray Baba Raba as a warrior. If his birth is placed in the early third century, the key moment of his career may be 235–238 C.E., when outside tribes (Romans, Ishmaelites, Byzantines, and Jews according to Stenhouse)[23] were threatening. He may have fought with Ishmaelites (Arabs) and Jews, but not likely with Romans. Abu'l Fath tells of a Jewish plot to kill him because of his success in talking officials out of taxing the Samaritans. The officials, rather than facing Baba directly, induced the Jews to kill him, promising that they would help rebuild the Jerusalem temple. As often happens in Samaritan stories, rescue comes from an outsider, this time a Jewish woman who revealed the plot to her Samaritan friends. Baba was not only saved, but he led his people in a massacre of Jews.

According to Samaritan tradition, Baba Raba spent the last years of his life under house arrest in Constantinople after being invited there by the emperor. His son Levi accompanied him, but was with him only a short time before Baba died of an illness at a young age.

---

[21] For example, Paul Stenhouse, "Baba Raba," in *A Companion to Samaritan Studies* (ed. A. Crown, R. Pummer, and A. Tal; Tübingen: Mohr, 1993), 38; and Montgomery, *Samaritans*, 102.

[22] Alan Crown, "The Samaritans in the Byzantine Orbit," *BJRL* 69 (1986): 124.

[23] Stenhouse, "Baba Raba," 37.

Amram Dare

Amram Dare plays the "Isaac" role in linking the two great Samaritan "patriarchs," Baba Raba and Marqe. A contemporary of Baba Raba, and a member of the council, he was the father of Marqe. His own important contributions include hymns that defined the genre for generations to come. Perhaps inspired by the Psalms of the Hebrew Bible and earlier Samaritan works, he is the first of the recorded Samaritan poets. His widely imitated poetry is referred to as a string of pearls *(Durran)* and twenty-eight of them appear in the Samaritan prayer book, the *Defter.* The absence of rhyme, a fixed number of lines in a verse, and a set number of words per line are characteristics of his work. Unlike biblical scribes and later Samaritan poets, he avoids acrostics. Various nuances of fourth-century Samaritan theology can be deduced from his work, particularly views of the attributes of God and early indications of such Samaritan practices as the intercalation of the calendar to establish the dates of festivals. The *Defter,* the basic Samaritan prayer book, as well as other liturgical works that focus on particular holy days like Passover and Pentecost facilitate our knowledge of the evolution of the liturgy and give many clues to the ritual and beliefs of the Samaritans.[24]

Marqe

The theological high point of the Samaritan renaissance in Byzantine times appears in the work of Marqe, who like his father was an able poet, capable of rich imagery and control of appropriate forms. His poems were longer than his father's, and never used the form *(Durran)* named after his father. His poems were usually of four or seven lines, and at least one acrostic survives among his works. His great work is the *Memar Marqah (Tibat Marqe)* a pedagogical commentary on various portions of the Pentateuch. This work, "Sayings of Marqah," a series of sermons expounding Samaritan theological beliefs, betrays several periods of Aramaic linguistic usage, and so the work obviously grew over the centuries, even if its core is from Marqe. It is divided into six parts. The first five parts expand on biblical stories and develop homilies on biblical verses. The last section is a midrash on the letters of the Hebrew alphabet, though essays on only twelve letters remain.[25] Samaritans venerate Marqe most highly of all nonbiblical personages, and later tradition describes him as a priest. MacDonald notes the assimilation of

---

[24] See Arthur E. Cowley, *The Samaritan Liturgy* (Oxford: Oxford University Press, 1909).
[25] For a summary of these sections, see Abraham Tal, "Samaritan Literature," in *The Samaritans* (ed. A. Crown. Tübingen: Mohr, 1989), 462–65.

Christian concepts in this work, particularly the attribution to Moses of traits that the gospel of John uses to describe Jesus.[26] The work becomes esoteric and kabbalistically inclined, hunting for secret meanings in certain combinations of letters. It is said that before Marqe's birth an angel appeared to his father, Amram, in a dream and instructed him to name the child Moses. The people felt that this was inappropriate, so he was named Marqe, a name with the same numerical value.[27]

PERSECUTION

The increasing visibility of the Samaritans during their religious revival made them an easy target for persecution. Unlike the Romans, the Byzantines more frequently distinguished between Jews and Samaritans and treated the latter much more harshly. Part of the Byzantine concern was the association of Samaritans with Gnosticism and its basic tenet that anything material was evil. The Eastern Church was in the midst of the Arian and Nestorian controversies concerning whether or not Jesus Christ was of the same substance as God the Father, and how the human nature or substance of Jesus related to his divine nature or substance. However much they differed on details, most Christians agreed that Jesus had a human nature, thus repudiating Christian Gnosticism, that is, the belief that Jesus was only spirit and lacked a physical body. Gnosticism had touched the Samaritan view of the material world. Some say that Simon Magus was a Samaritan leader and instrumental in the introduction of Gnosticism.[28] Any hint of this heresy was a threat to the orthodoxy of the Byzantines.

Byzantine animosity toward the Samaritans also had a practical side. The Samaritans owned such prime holy places as Jacob's well and Joseph's tomb, potential prizes as Byzantine Christianity made greater inroads into the Holy Land. No wonder that when Byzantine forces arrived in the vicinity of Mount Gerizim and assumed near proprietorship of these sites, tensions with the local inhabitants intensified. In 415 tempers flared among the helpless Samaritans as a Byzantine expedition dug for the bones of Joseph at Shechem. This was followed by a Byzantine excavation in 450–451 at Awerta, the supposed burial site of the Aaronite priests Eleazar, Ithamar, and Pinhas.

---

[26] John MacDonald, *Memar Marqah* (Berlin: Töpelmann, 1963), xvii–xix.

[27] Peterman as cited by Montgomery, *Samaritans,* 294.

[28] A recent evaluation of Simon is made in Florent Heintz, *Actes 8,5–25 et l'accusation de magie contre les prophètes thaumaturges dans l'antiquité* (Paris: Gabalda, 1997).

Tension grew as the theological struggles regarding the nature of Christ went beyond the bounds of the church councils at Nicea, Ephesus, and Chalcedon and were manifest in inter-Christian political struggles. Jerusalem came under the episcopacy of Theodosius, a Monophysite (believing in one divine nature in Jesus in defiance of the Orthodox councils) who set off a bitter struggle among Christian factions in Palestine. The Samaritans encouraged and exploited the struggle, joining in the destruction of property of Christians on each side of the controversy and earning the deep enmity of all sides.

Occasionally, official government documents offer a glimpse into the fate of the Samaritans, usually indicating restrictions that are placed upon them. In the earliest remaining Roman document, the emperor Theodosius (379–395) addresses the governor of Alexandria, a seaport with a sizable Samaritan population. He decrees that, while individuals may be taxed according to their means to support the imperial fleet, the community of Jews or Samaritans may not be so taxed because the burden would then fall as heavily on the poor as on the rich.[29]

Offending the Christian majority was impolitic, however. During the fourth century, Christianity had been transformed from a persecuted minority to a formidable political power and sought to hold the threatening minorities at bay with various preemptive and retaliatory strategies. Like the Jews, the Samaritans were forbidden to hold civil service jobs.[30] Honorius (the western Roman emperor who ruled in Ravenna 395–423 C.E.) deprived Jews and Samaritans of the privilege of being royal informers. His counterpart in Constantinople, Theodosius II (408–450), facilitated the conversion of Samaritans to Christianity by ruling in 426 that no Jewish or Samaritan child could be disinherited on account of conversion. In 439, he rescinded all laws that had permitted Jews, Samaritans, pagans, "and other heretics" to hold certain offices and honors that would put them in a position to harm Christians.[31]

Rebellion peaked in the great confrontation of 484, the immediate cause of which is elusive. Presumably the Samaritans (like other groups) believed Zeno's (emperor, 474–491) position to be vulnerable. They already feared that Orthodox Christians intended to build a church on Mount Gerizim as part of their continuing usurpation of the Holy Land. The Samaritans may also have hoped for aid from nonOrthodox (Monophysite) Christians. In any case, Procopius[32] tells us that the Samaritans attacked the

---

[29] Montgomery, *Samaritans,* 105–6.
[30] Montgomery, *Samaritans,* 108.
[31] Montgomery, *Samaritans,* 109–10.
[32] Procopius, *Buildings* 5.7.

Church of St. Stephen at Nablus during a celebration of Pentecost and cut off the presiding bishop's fingers. They proceeded to Caesarea and proclaimed Justus, a Samaritan, political leader and then massacred Christians. According to the *Samaritan Chronicles,* Zeno retaliated by coming to Nablus, executing many leaders of the community, and offering the rest a choice between conversion and martyrdom. A Samaritan synagogue became a convent, and the Church of St. Mary was built on the probable site of the chief Samaritan sanctuary.

Possible Samaritan ruins and ruins of later St. Mary's Church on Mount Gerizim.
Photo by Terry Giles.

Procopius describes yet another fifth-century rebellion by the Samaritans[33] during the reign of Zeno's successor, Anastasius (491–518). An attack party scaled an unfortified cliff, fell upon the guards on Mount Gerizim, and slaughtered them. However, they apparently had little support from the intimidated residents of the village below and soon succumbed to the garrison at Nablus.

Rural Samaritans developed a reputation as highway robbers and fake converts. Contemporary analyses of powerless peasant groups lead one to ex-

---

[33] Procopius, *Buildings* 5.7.

pect such survival tactics.[34] Dominic Crossan has recently utilized social history, particularly the work of Eric Hobsbawm,[35] to illuminate banditry in first-century Palestine. The same dynamics probably operated later in the region as well. Social banditry develops in an agricultural, peasant society as a way for otherwise powerless people to make a bid for power. Remnants of Samaritan synagogues suggest gradually diminishing prosperity until the time of Justinian, thus confirming this reconstruction of Samaritan society, at least in a general way.

When Justinian (527–565) assumed the Byzantine throne in 527, he reiterated the laws excluding Samaritans from certain offices. He also included the Samaritans with Jews and pagans in a set of laws that safeguarded hereditary rights of Christian children of these groups and essentially precluded the possibility of Samaritans owning real estate.[36]

Justinian also initiated the most far-reaching legislation against the Samaritans. At first, he included them with Jews and pagans. The ensuing Samaritan rebellion (in 529) provoked not only military response from the emperor but also new legislation. Henceforth, Samaritan converts must demonstrate their sincerity. They could not inherit any goods, and their synagogues were to be destroyed. Although some other groups were similarly interdicted, Jews were not. Likewise, Jews were exempt from laws in 531 that prohibited Samaritans (along with radical Christian groups) from testifying against Christians or even against members of their own community. In 537 the Samaritans were included with Jews and pagans in a reiteration of the edicts of Theodosius II.

The legal position of the Samaritans grew even worse under Justin II (565–578), who essentially outlawed the sect in 572. Its members could not serve in any governmental capacity, go to court, hold Christian slaves, or receive education.

The repeated rebellions of the sixth century eventually spelled the virtual doom of the Samaritan community. Alan Crown has made the account of the origins of the riots by John Malalas available in English.[37] An episode of jealousy at a chariot race in 529 triggered widespread slaughter first of Christians by Samaritans, but then of Samaritans by Christians. Five new, heavily protected churches arose on Mount Gerizim. In 556 a second wave of Christian anger led to the slaughter of many more Samaritans. Already decimated by an intervening plague in 544 that reappeared in 556, the Samaritan population and its major architectural artifacts virtually disappeared. In

---

[34] Procopius, *Buildings* 5.114; and *m. Pe'ah* 2.7.
[35] John D. Crossan, *The Historical Jesus* (San Francisco: Harper, 1991), 168–69.
[36] Montgomery, *Samaritans,* 114.
[37] Alan D. Crown, "Samaritans in the Byzantine Orbit," 133–34.

572 Justin II administered a coup de grâce with his reenactment of the anti-Samaritan prohibitions of 527. Members of the sect could not serve in any governmental capacity, go to court, or attend school.[38] They could not hold Christian slaves, and the authorities monitored the authenticity of their conversions. All of this legislation put strong pressure on them to convert to Christianity. Many centuries remain almost blank in the Samaritan chronicles.

During these periods of oppression, the Samaritans, like the Jews, often fled, and colonies of Samaritans, with a total population estimated at 150,000, appeared throughout the Middle East (notably at Aleppo, Tyre, Caesarea, Ascalon, Gaza, Damascus, and Cairo) and elsewhere in the Mediterranean world. Evidence of Samaritan communities has come to light at Carthage, Delos, Constantinople, Thasos, Thessalonica, Rhodes, Ravenna, Rome, and other Italian cities. Samaritans lived as merchants, craftsmen (e.g., weavers or glass blowers), and administrators.

However, flight was no long-term escape from Christianity, which had quickly filled the vacuum resulting from the collapse of the Roman Empire and its attendant state religion. To a greater degree than Jews, Samaritans faced discriminatory legislation and practice throughout the empire. Thus many who left Palestine, like those who remained, converted to Christianity or at least assumed Christian names in order to avoid persecution and gain advancement in government and even in the church.[39] Converts knew that Christians would question the authenticity of their conversions. This was a legacy of Justin's paradoxical strategy to woo or coerce Monophysite Christians especially and all his other subjects into accepting Orthodoxy. The empire was ambivalent about assimilating these Semitic peoples, on both religious and cultural grounds (compare the case, a millennium later, of the Spanish Inquisition's efforts at assimilating Jews and Muslims). Still, when exposed, many Samaritans found that they could maintain their office by paying bribes to the Byzantine leaders.[40] Most simply merged into the majority culture.

Precluded from many vocational options and victims of unfavorable inheritance laws, the Samaritans slid down the social ladder into a basically agrarian life with all the accompanying lack of power and economic security. Their increasing poverty occasionally elicited sympathy from the government. As mentioned, Theodosius exempted the Samaritan synagogues from the obligation to supply ships to the navy. He also protected the Samaritans

---

[38] Montgomery, *Samaritans,* 122.
[39] Stenhouse, *The Kitab al Tarikh of Abu'l Fath,* 199.
[40] Alan D. Crown, "Samaritans in the Byzantine Orbit," 119.

in a spat with the Christians over Mount Gerizim (which Abu'l Fath mentions as well).[41]

Conformity was the major response to this legal repression, but there were other options, including rebellions and flight to more comfortable locations.[42] Their religion, as a source of both strength and oppression, became a preoccupation. Although some abandoned it, those who wanted to defend it became increasingly serious about defining the faith that they were ready to defend. The pressure was to establish a united orthodoxy.

---

[41] Montgomery, *Samaritans,* 106.

[42] Reinhard Pummer ("The Samaritans in Egypt," in *Études sémitiques et samaritaines* [ed. Christian-Bernard Amphoux, Albert Frey, and Ursala Schattner-Rieser; Histoire du texte biblique 4; Lausanne: Éditions du Zèbre, 1998], 218) cites two papyri evidencing Samaritan presence in Egypt in the fifth and sixth centuries.

Chapter 6

Islamic Invasion to the Renaissance

THE ISLAMIC PERIOD

When the Muslims swept across the Middle East in the seventh century, the Samaritans, not surprisingly, colluded with them in the takeover of Palestine. Samaritan men were sometimes unwilling conscripts in Muslim armies, but often they willingly formed a fifth column of guides and spies (developed in subcultures of banditry?), thereby facilitating the Muslim invasion. Palestinian towns with large Samaritan populations were among the first to fall to the Muslims. Samaritans preferred the Muslim devil they did not know to the Christian devil they did. In return they not only escaped Byzantine oppression but also received temporary tax benefits and religious freedom.

Relationships with the Muslims were generally less oppressive than those with the Byzantine Christians. Some Samaritans even reached high office. In the tenth century, the Fatimid khalif of Egypt appointed a Samaritan, Hatakvi ben Isaak, governor of first northern and then southern Palestine, initiating a period of Samaritan participation in government. In the eleventh century, a Samaritan, Ab Hasda, served as inquisitor of Palestine at Caesarea and Akko. This apparent Samaritan partial assimilation may be reflected in the group's use of Arabic as its both literary and spoken language. Still, assimilation was never extensive, and at times the Samaritans were known as *Lamasasiah* (the "Don't Touch"-ers), an exclamation some would express to non-Samaritans who approached them.

A Samaritan astrologer approached Muhammed and elicited the following covenant from him: "I Muhammed bin Muttalib, have commanded that a treaty of peace and security be written down for the Samaritans concerning themselves and their families and their property and houses of worship and religious endowments through all my realm and in all their territories. And that this be effective for them and as a covenant of peace among the people of Palestine; and as a safe conduct."

Abu'l Fath, *The Kitab al Tarikh* (trans. and ed. Paul Stenhouse; Sydney: Mandelbaum Trust, University of Sydney, 1985), 245.

The initial beneficence of the Muslims was short-lived. Religious oppression was slow to come, but since the Muslims were not convinced that the Samaritans were a "people of the Book," they taxed them even more than Christians and Jews. High taxation was particularly oppressive during the reign of the Umayyad khalif Yazzid (680–683) and the Abbasid khalif el-Mu'tasim (833–842). (Precise tax records from the sixteenth century help us estimate the number of Samaritans in the Ottoman Empire, although census records are less ample earlier.)[1] Samaritans lost land under the khalif Harun ar-Rashid (764–809), and later el-Amin (809–813) sanctioned the burning of several Samaritan synagogues. The tomb of the high priest Nethanel was destroyed by al-Mutawakkil (847–861), and one of his governors apparently sought to outlaw Samaritanism. With heavy taxation and limited access to the ruling elites, the Samaritans again found themselves needing to choose among the options of conformity, rebellion, flight, conversion, and religious reform. Through it all, their spiral into poverty continued.

In 754, during the reign of the Abbasid khalif al-Mansour (754–775), the Muslims triggered the first Samaritan civil violence in the Islamic period. A Muslim force raided Mount Gerizim and desecrated the Byzantine Christian monuments there. They burned the tomb of Zeno and destroyed the churches and cemeteries. The Samaritans exploited the opportunity by killing some Christians, a strike at past Byzantine injustice. The Muslim government did not applaud but extorted the cost of the sortie from the Samaritans, holding their high priest hostage until a sum was paid.

The increased political turmoil and oppression encouraged widespread conversion to Islam and stimulated migration to urban centers in the Middle East. Communities developed at Aleppo, Tyre, Caesarea, Ascalon, Gaza, Damascus, and Cairo. Benjamin of Tudela in the 1170s counted one thousand Samaritans in Nablus, three hundred in Ascalon, two hundred in Caesarea, and four hundred in Damascus. By 636 all of these cities had come under Muslim rule.

Although Samaritans paid special taxes because of their religion and subsequently found themselves targets of persecution, their practice of religion was initially tolerated, and this allowed a brief and limited renaissance in the early Muslim period. The high priest of the Samaritan community reestablished the council of sages in 639 with the sanction of Muhammed's friend and the first Muslim khalif, Abu Bakr.

The earliest tensions for the Samaritans in Islamic times occurred within the sect itself. In the middle of the eighth century a dispute over the selection

---

[1] Benjamin Z. Kedar, "The Frankish Period," in *The Samaritans* (ed. Alan Crown; Tübingen: Mohr, 1989), 82.

of a high priest created a schism, probably a resurfacing of the tension between orthodox and Dosithean groups. The conflict intensified when each
side chose an alternate way of determining the religious calendar. There are
indications that the orthodox group convinced the Muslims to outlaw the
Dositheans.

The early Muslim period also witnessed a resurgence of Samaritan
scholarship. The Pentateuch probably was translated into Arabic in the eleventh century, with its classic formulation attributed to Abu'l Said in the thirteenth century. A lively debate arose focusing on a new punctuation system
introduced in Ascalon in 1139, and the *Tulida,* a book of genealogies, was
begun. Many pentateuchal scrolls were written during the twelfth century in
Nablus and possibly in Damascus. Surviving manuscripts are cited in the catalogues of von Gall and Ben Zvi.

The Samaritans adopted the Arabic language for daily use and incorporated many Muslim ideas in their theology and liturgy. By the seventh
century, the Samaritans were too small a minority to influence Islam signifi-
cantly. Some motifs, like depictions of the day of judgment that appear in the
Memar Marqah, have notable parallels in the *Qur'an* and could imply Samaritan influence in Islamic thought, but the direction of the flow of influence is
not always obvious. Islam affected the Samaritans profoundly. Elah, a close
parallel to Allah, became the preferred divine name. They began using part of
the Muslim creed, "There is no God, but God." And they introduced prayers
and other statements with the Muslim form "In the name of God."

A "day of judgment" is a common theme among the descendants of the Israelite faith: Judaism, Christianity, and Islam. It derives from, but is not the equivalent to, the "Day of the
Lord (Yahweh)." There are scholarly differences, but a general pattern emerges. Amos
5:18–20 is probably the earliest reference. It implies an earlier positive anticipation of the
Day of the Lord, perhaps rooted in cosmic war imagery that later becomes incorporated in
the cult. Amos says that the Day of the Lord will not be a moment of victory, but of judgment. These twin themes of victory and judgment continue through the Hebraic tradition
with increasing eschatological overtones and are manifest in the literature of the Samaritans as well as in the larger faiths.

Unlike the Byzantine period, when the government persecuted the community, much Samaritan suffering in the Muslim period was incidental.
Christians, Jews, and Samaritans suffered alike in the Muslim civil wars,
whose battlefields were often in towns they inhabited. Famine and then bu-
bonic plague also befell them. The loss of land was probably a significant step
in the movement from farm to city, from a large but poor population to near
extinction during the Middle Ages.

THE CRUSADES

On July 11, 1099, the Crusaders Tancred and Eustache of Boulogne arrived in Nablus seeking supplies for their troops poised to take Jerusalem. Although they extorted considerable supplies, the presence of many Christians in Nablus dissuaded them from sacking the town. That episode set the tone for the fate of the Samaritans at the hands of the Crusaders. Some of their buildings were destroyed in the initial attacks, but the group's docility led the Europeans to leave them essentially unharmed. They may have owed their good fortune to their small number (probably less than ten percent of the population even of Nablus), the Crusaders' desire for peace, and perhaps even a Crusader enchantment with the story of the Good Samaritan. The Crusaders left their mark by converting the Samaritan synagogue at Nablus into a church (the tower of which still survives) and, somewhat more literally, in the casual incision of a cross in the shield-shaped *ayin* of a Samaritan inscription.

A few Samaritans still lived throughout cities of the Levant, as well as Damascus and Cairo,[2] but most Samaritans now lived in Nablus and probably numbered a few thousand. Three experiences of affliction particularly stand out during this period. In 1137 an army from Damascus staged one of many Muslim attacks on the weakly fortified city of Nablus, killing some and taking five hundred Samaritans as captives. A wealthy Samaritan from Acre paid their ransom. In 1184 Saladin's troops raided Nablus and, according to the reports, deported many Frankish and Samaritan prisoners to Damascus. In the 1242 the Knights Templar raided the city, killing many and selling others in the Acre slave market. They were finally forced to retreat before the Ayyubid force.

Samaritans often distinguished themselves among their conquerors. They excelled in medicine, for example, and Samaritan physicians are listed along with Jews, Syrians, and Saracens as the Franks' doctors of choice. The Crusaders may even have used Abu Ishaq Ibrahim, a Samaritan physician to Saladin, sultan of Egypt and chief opponent of the Crusaders.

When the Muslims returned to power in 1244, they converted the synagogue/church of Nablus into a mosque, and in subsequent centuries the Samaritans enjoyed varying degrees of access to their central city. They continued to suffer attacks by Muslims and Mongols and finally Mamluks, who destroyed many coastal cities to foil Italian fleets. Only Gaza remained a significant port and an important Samaritan center.

---

[2] Pummer ("Samaritans in Egypt," 218) cites a 1038 document demonstrating the existence of a Samaritan community in Cairo.

Whatever the tensions with the Muslims, this was a period of relative peace between Jews and Samaritans. For example, the Samaritan Aaron b. Manir, a hymnist of thirteenth-century Damascus, utilized the 613 precepts of Maimonides as a model for one of his works, reflecting a period when the Samaritan community profited from its relationship with Judaism. Similar cooperation prevailed in Cairo, where Jews and Samaritans were buried in the same cemetery and signed one another's contracts.[3]

The Jewish scholar Maimonides (ca. 1135–1204) made a list of the 613 precepts or commandments found in the Torah and introduced them with an essay on the criteria by which they are chosen. Two Samaritan documents enumerate the same number of precepts. The first is the "Song of the Precepts" by Aaron ben Manir in the thirteenth century, and the second is the *Sayr al-Qalb* of Abraham ha-Qabasi in the mid-sixteenth century. Six hundred thirteen is not an obvious number and suggests some relationship between the two communities. Both of these works were written in Damascus, an asylum for Jews as well as Samaritans. Jews fleeing Spain probably brought the work of Maimonides to Damascus, where relatively congenial relations, at least, existed between Jews and Samaritans and the 613 precepts thus made their way into Samaritan tradition.

THE RENAISSANCE

Our sources become much richer during the period of the Renaissance. The Samaritans come into focus through the eyes of Christian, Jewish, and Muslim travelers who left accounts of their passage through cities inhabited by Samaritans. Usually these accounts tell us more about the cities than about the Samaritans, and often they provide only the slightest description of Samaritan life. Nevertheless, such accounts give our best clues as to the number and location of Samaritans in different places.

Beginning in the twelfth century, we have the comments on Samaritan customs by Benjamin of Tudela, followed in the next century by a description of Nablus by the Muslim geographer Yakut,[4] whose colleagues of the fourteenth century, Dimashki and Abul Fida, offered similar descriptions. Yakut said,

Nablus is inhabited by the Samaritans, who live in this place alone, and only go elsewhere for the purpose of trade and advantage. The Samaritans are a sect of the Jews. They have a large mosque in Nablus which they call Al Kuds—The

---

[3] Pummer, "Samaritans in Egypt," 220.
[4] Dated 1225 according to Montgomery, *Samaritans,* 136.

Holy City—and the Holy City of Jerusalem is accursed by them, and when one of them is forced to go there he takes a stone and throws it against the city of Jerusalem. . . . There is a spring in a cave which they visit and venerate and for this reason it is that there are so many Samaritans in the city of Nablus.[5]

The itinerant Ibn Batutta also described Nablus in the fourteenth century, particularly its crops. In the same century several Europeans began recording impressions of Samaritans and their territories. The Italian Franciscan Niccolo Poggibonsi mentioned the presence of Samaritans in Sebaste and Cairo. The German friar Wilhelm Von Boldensole recorded comments on Samaritan beliefs:

> Here [in Nablus] lives a curious community, called Samaritans. They do not follow the rites of the Christians, nor those of the Jews, nor those of the Saracens or the pagans. Though they believe in one God, they have quite unusual teachings and rules and regard themselves as the only righteous ones and the only true believers in God and differ also in their dress from the other people of these parts; while the Christians wind yellow linen sheets round their heads, the Saracens white ones, and the Jews blue ones, they dress in red cloth.[6]

This attire followed a dress code imposed by the Muslims.

Simon Sigoli of Florence noticed Samaritans in Alexandria, and his companion Gucci leaves a description of Nablus. A French nobleman, Ogier d'Anglure, met members of the sect in Gaza. They all described a beautiful and productive Nablus, abundant in olive oil and carob, where a diminished community of Samaritans lived in relative tranquility under the Mamluks. In 1316 that peace evaporated when the inhabitants of Nablus instigated a brief rebellion against the Muslim officials, an act that lessened the Samaritans' sense of security for the rest of the century. The insurrection quickly collapsed, but it provoked a series of Muslim military ventures throughout Palestine which, in turn, accelerated the dispersal of peoples, including the Samaritans, during the latter part of the century.

During the first half of the fourteenth century, Damascus was the favorite city of such emigres, and all indications are that it was a hospitable city. The Samaritans built a synagogue that they called by the same name as one of the synagogues of Nablus, Knesset Haaben.[7] They had their own high priest, Ithamar b. Aaron, scion of a long priestly line that had separated from the Nablus priests in the thirteenth century, although his immediate predecessors

---

[5] Guy Le Strange, *Palestine under the Muslims* (London: 1890), 512–13; cited in Nathan Schur, *History of the Samaritans* (BEATAJ 18; New York: Lang, 1989), 104.

[6] Wilhelm von Boldensele in F. Khull, *Zweier Deutscher Ordensleute Pilgerfahrten nach Jerusalem* (Graz: Styria, 1895), 40–41. Cited by Schur, *History of the Samaritans,* 108.

[7] Itzak Ben Zvi, "Migginze Shomron," *Sinai* 12 (1943): 410–17.

do not appear in any extant documents. Ithamar led the community from 1343 to 1362, the length of his tenure implying amity both within the Samaritan community and between it and the wider population. A comfortable cultural context also explains why most surviving Samaritan pentateuchal manuscripts from the first half of the fourteenth century come from Damascus. Apart from the priestly families, the most visible families in Damascus were the Pigma, Ikkara, and Segiana, the last two of which also resided in Egypt and Gaza.

Historically, Cairo shared with Damascus a reputation as a major refuge for Samaritans, but in the early fourteenth century, it was not very hospitable to Christians and Jews and presumably Samaritans. Few documents specifically mention Samaritans, though they were often subsumed under the category of Jews. Persecutions of Christians and Jews in 1301 and 1321 probably included Samaritans and other minorities as well. A fire in Cairo in 1320 unleashed strong anti-Christian and anti-Jewish reactions that the sultan, Malik al-Nasir, tried to control. Such hostile sentiments and actions were absent in Damascus. Both communities experienced relative international tranquility in the early half of the fourteenth century, resulting from a treaty of 1322 between the Mamluks and their major adversaries, the Mongols.

Although the Samaritan population was relatively small (the Arab geographer Dimashki found only one hundred in Palestine), the fourteenth century witnessed a new surge of theological and literary activity growing out of a reconciliation among several Samaritan sects, particularly the priestly-centered orthodox and the more lay-oriented Dositheans. This irenic spirit finds expression in a number of works. The high priest Pinhas b. Joseph b. Ozzi b. Netanel b. Pinhas b. Eleazar (1308–1367) inspired and orchestrated a renaissance motivated in large part by apprehension that their small community might disappear unless it could stem the conversions to Islam.

A key document stemming from this renaissance was the Abisha scroll, the revered copy of the Pentateuch discovered on the feast of Simhat Torah, 1355. It became the central religious artifact of the community. Its sanctity derives from the tradition (and the acrostic contained within the text of Deuteronomy) attributing it to Abisha, the great-grandnephew of Moses. Scholars are skeptical, although its actual origin is not obvious. Much of the manuscript was older, but some portions probably come from the fourteenth century as part of a restoration of the manuscript. The first reference to it appears as a marginal note on a manuscript of the *Tulida*. The scroll may have been in Egypt at one time, but strong sanctions against even the priests leaving the Holy Land make that seem doubtful. Some suspect that the high priest Pinhas b. Joseph b. Ozzi b. Netanel b. Pinhas b. Eleazar contrived to have the chronicler Abu'l Fath find it to reinforce the former's claim to

Samaritan priest with ancient scroll of the Torah. *Photo by Robert T. Anderson*

the priesthood.[8] It is this manuscript that E. K. Warren persuaded the Samaritans to have photographed in hopes that its sale would be a financial boon to them. The brass scroll case in the Chamberlain-Warren collection may have housed this manuscript at one time.

Several Samaritan interpretations of various parts of their history originate in Islamic times, especially during the time of the high priest Pinhas. In 1355 he commissioned Abu'l Fath of the Danafite family to write a history of the Samaritans as part of a new blossoming of the community. His work, the

---

[8] Alan Crown, "The Abisha Scroll of the Samaritans," *BJRL* 58 (1975): 64.

Kitab at-Tarikh, is the most helpful of the documents available. The pre-served manuscript may display the handwriting of as many as nine different copyists, and it reflects a conciliatory spirit uniting orthodox and Dosithean, priestly and lay, positions. Abu'l Fath certainly played an active role in Pinhas's renaissance, though curiously little biographical evidence surfaces for either man in other manuscripts. The core of another work, *The Book of Joshua,* a historical commentary on the period from Moses to Alexander with parallels to the biblical books and, according to Bowman,[9] reflecting views of an opponent of the priests (Dosithean?), also dates to in this century (if not the one before). From their renewed base of authority, the priests maintained their old powers but were more open to heterodox viewpoints.

"The Samaritan *Book of Joshua* is not Scripture, but more of an interpretive chronicle. This is the account of Joshua's death: Joshua, the son of Nun reigned for forty-five years. At the approach of his death, he assembled the Israelites and made a covenant with them to ob-serve that which Moses the Prophet, upon whom be peace, had codified. He then offered sacrifices on his own behalf and on theirs and bid them farewell, and in general did approxi-mately the same things as those done by our master Moses the Prophet, upon him be peace, when he bade (the people) farewell. He moreover chose twelve chieftains from all the nine and a half tribes, for whom he drew lots in the presence of the entire assembly of Israel in the meadow of al-Baha, after having tested their knowledge and ability. The lot of kingship fell to a certain 'Abil, the son of the brother of Caleb, of the tribe of Judah. Joshua consequently girded him with the royal and judicial authority, invested him with the crown, and called upon the assembly to obey his commands. 'Abil himself he bade render obedi-ence to the Priest, keep him informed about all his affairs, and set no undertaking in motion without letting him know of it first. Thereupon Joshua the son of Nun, upon whom be peace, died and was buried in Kafr Ghuwaira."

John Bowman, *Samaritan Documents Relating to Their History, Religion, and Life* (Pittsburgh: Pickwick, 1977), 73–74.

Only a decade before, Jacob b. Ishmael had updated the brief *Tulida (Genealogy)* that Eleazar b. Amram compiled in 1149. It listed the genealo-gies from Adam to Moses, then from Aaron to Ozzi, and continued the list of high priests and important Samaritan families. The related *Salsala* or *Chain* (of priests), compiled by the high priest Jacob b. Aaron, brings the list down to the twentieth century.

Tabia and/or Pinhas extended Abu'l Fath's work with materials from the Jewish Bible in what comes to be known as *Chronicle II* later in the fourteenth

---

[9] John Bowman, *The Samaritan Problem* (Pittsburg: Pickwick, 1975), 18.

century. There are two other chronicles of considerably less significance. One is the *Asatir*, recounting the time from Adam to Moses, and concentrating especially on Moses stories. The other is the so-called *New Chronicle* or *Chronicle Adler*, which draws from the *Tulida* and Abu'l Fath.

Other scholars were also at work. Pinhas b. Joseph (1308–1367) revived the Samaritan *piyyutim* (prayers), written in Hebrew. His son Abisha "Ba'al ha-memar" wrote many poems included in the liturgy. Matanah Hamazri worked in Cairo, and Aaron b. Manir in Damascus. Another son of Pinhas, Eleazar b. Pinhas (priest 1363–1387), wrote a Hebrew grammar.

By midcentury population gradually shifted from Damascus toward Egypt. Plague and earthquakes had ravished Syria, and provisions were extremely scarce. In addition minorities faced regulations directed against them in midcentury, including sumptuary laws prescribing that only Muslims could wear white turbans, Christians blue, Jews yellow, and Samaritans red. Further, non-Muslims could not ride horses, pray aloud, or appear unmarked in public baths. Movement was a predictable response to such laws.

Some families who moved from Palestine or Syria gravitated to Gaza, a city consistently praised by travelers of the time. The ubiquitous Haseburai and Ikkara families produced several Pentateuchs about midcentury in nearby Gerar, on the Egyptian border. Easy movement among Samaritan communities is evidenced by three scribes, two in Damascus (the high priest and perhaps his nephew) and a member of the Ikkara family in Gerar, collaborating on the same manuscript. Other evidence indicates that the Damascene priest Abd Yahweh b. Berakhah spent some time in Nablus during the same period.

Many Samaritans continued on to Egypt, where, as in Syria and elsewhere, they became affluent and found government jobs.[10] A Samaritan synagogue is identified on Darb al-Kurani Street in the Harat al-Zuwailah section.[11] Their presence can be documented both from the reports of travelers and from the manuscripts they produced. In the first half of the fourteenth century Samaritan manuscript production was limited almost exclusively to Damascus. Later on in the fourteenth century, this activity was about equally distributed between Damascus and Egypt. The major Samaritan migrations seem to predate the economic crisis that occurred between 1384 and 1408 in connection with a diminished silver reserve and the devaluation of the dirham,[12] which affected all parts of the Mamluk empire equally.

---

[10] Bertold Spuler, *The Muslim World* (Leiden: Brill, 1967), 2:58.

[11] Pummer, "Samaritan Material Remains and Archaeology," 225.

[12] Abraham N. Poliak, *Feudalism in Egypt, Syria, Palestine, and Lebanon, 1250–1900* (Philadelphia: Porcupine Press, 1939; repr., 1977), 66.

In the fifteenth century, descriptions of Samaritans appear in the works of Francesco Suriano (an Italian monk and head of the Franciscans in Jerusalem),[13] Martin Kabatnik (a Czech who visited Nablus and Egypt), several Jewish travelers, an anonymous traveler from Candia to Gaza, one Meshulla traveling from Volterra in Italy to Gaza and Egypt, and Rabbi Ovadia of Bartinoro touring the same area. All these comment briefly on the number of Samaritans, their relative prosperity, and their dress.

At the turn of the century, Mongol troops under Tamerlane sacked Damascus and deported many of the city's artisans to Samarkand. This was a serious blow to the prosperity of Damascus, from which it never fully recovered. Christians and other minority groups welcomed the Mongols as deliverers. The fact that Samaritans continued to produce manuscripts in Damascus during this period suggests that they preferred the Mongols to the Muslims. The Mongols did practice religious toleration and protected many groups. Samaritans also may have preferred Syria to Egypt because the latter suffered a devastating drought in 1403 with subsequent famine, plague, and high prices.

The death of Tamerlane in 1405 allowed Egypt to reassert its control over Damascus. But Egypt itself saw serious trouble with civil war among the Mamluks, other internal insurrections, and outside attacks from Cyprus and the Mongols. Samaritan manuscript activity (and therefore witnesses to Samaritan inhabitants) ceased abruptly in Egypt during this time, but remained relatively normal in Damascus until the second quarter of the century.

Conditions in Palestine during the latter part of the fifteenth century were particularly cruel and surely contributed to further emigration. The plague struck with notable virulence in 1461, 1468, 1477, and 1491. Records state that the last outbreak took a toll of 130 persons per day in Jerusalem alone.[14] In addition, the winters of 1472 and 1492 were uncommonly severe. The latter felled 360 houses in Jerusalem. An earthquake also rocked Jerusalem in 1485. External and internal pressures added to the turmoil. Regular Bedouin raids on the cities climaxed in an attack on Jerusalem in 1480. When the forceful Kait Bey rose to power, he enforced new taxes on minorities like the Samaritans, Christians, and Jews. By the end of the century Jaffa, Caesarea, Sidon, Acre, and Bethlehem were in ruins. Jerusalem in 1484 had "many Saracen mosques, Jewish synagogues, and Samaritan tabernacles, but a great part of the city is laid waste, and the houses stand in ruins without inhabitants."[15]

---

[13] Schur, *History of the Samaritans,* 110.

[14] Jacob DeHaas, *History of Palestine: The Last Two Thousand Years* (New York: Macmillan, 1934), 18.

[15] DeHaas, *History of Palestine,* 321.

During this period the diaspora Samaritans come into sharp focus both from their own records and from those of tourists. A Jew, Meshullam b. Menahem, reports that fifty Samaritan heads of households lived in Egypt in 1480. Three years later, Obadiah of Bertinoro visited Cairo and also counted fifty Samaritan families, explaining that many of them were involved in business and government. Samaritans themselves were on the move. For example, the 1482 *tashqil* (a vertical note through the biblical text created by isolating certain letters of the text; see the page from Leviticus CW 2473) of the Barbarini triglot implies that one of the scribes, Ab Yetrana (Kapit), had left Damascus. In 1484 Jacob b. Matanah b. Abul Fath b. Abraham (Shafet) came from Shechem to Egypt and wrote a note in a Samaritan Pentateuch, Ben Zvi's *caph cheth*. Crown notes special scribal flowering among scribes of the Munis clan in Egypt in the mid- to late fifteenth century.[16]

In 1481, four Samaritan families resided in Gaza, a city Fabri described as a "dishful of butter," where the Gerah family was most prominent. It is said to be twice as populous as Jerusalem and noteworthy for its many palm trees, Christians, and air of tolerance.[17] In 1486, Masudi writes,

> The Samaritans inhabit the districts of Palestine and the Jordan, such as the well-known city [the text is blank, but presumably refers to Gaza] which is between Ramle and Tiberias, and other places, and finally the city of Nablus; but the most part of them live in the latter city.[18]

Our best indication of the size of the major Samaritan communities continues to be the volume of manuscript production, which was unusually high in the latter half of the fifteenth century. During the previous century and a half, leadership in this activity had alternated between Egypt and Damascus. An eleven-year period, 1474–1485, witnessed an unusually high number of manuscripts copied in both communities. In the two decades following 1490, however, production in Egypt declined.

The end of the century saw diaspora Samaritans commit extensive resources to the restoration of Nablus. In 1497 Ab Sehuta b. Sadaqah of Damascus and Jacob b. Abraham of Egypt repaired Synagogue Evil Yakov.[19] The following year a *mazba,* a small podium in the ark or niche that houses the Torah scroll in the front of the synagogue, was built in the synagogue at Nablus for the Abisha scroll.[20] The Safr, Shafet, Danfi, and priestly families

---

[16] Alan Crown, "Studies in Samaritan Scribal Practices and Manuscript History: I. Manuscript Prices and Values," *BJRL* 65 (1983): 72–94, esp. 76.

[17] DeHaas, *History of Palestine,* 301.

[18] Montgomery, *Samaritans,* 135.

[19] Yitzak Ben Zvi, "Migginze Shomron," *Sinai* 10 (1942): 100–106, esp. 101.

[20] J. E. H. Thomson, *The Samaritans: Their Testimony to the Religion of Israel* (London: Oliver and Boyd, 1919), 131.

of Nablus emerge from obscurity. A few years later, in 1509, a tapestry for the Abisha scroll was the gift of one Jacob b. Abraham b. Isaac (Metuhiah) of Damascus,[21] otherwise unknown.

In the sixteenth century Moshe Bassula and Juan Perera reported partial destruction of Nablus. The German Saloaman Schweigger and the Dutchman Johann van Kootwyk report much the same.

Relationships among Jews, Christians, and Samaritans seem to have been congenial at this time. Samaritans in Cairo accepted the authority of the Jewish rabbi, and the Jews of Nablus accepted the authority of the Samaritan high priest.[22] In 1497 two Christians witnessed the sale of von Gall's Pentateuch A. The easy intercourse between Samaritans and Jews outside Nablus may have expedited the development of minuscule writing in Damascus and Egypt.[23]

In 1513 the second part of the *Book of Joshua,* later obtained by Scaliger (the first part dating from 1362–1363), was completed, and in 1515 Pinhas restored the manuscript now known as Ben Zvi 10. Pinhas claimed it as a manuscript he had written, thus inflating his record; this practice may have been widespread.

The sixteenth century had hardly begun before the Mamluks gave way to the Ottoman Turks. By 1516 Selim I, the Ferocious, had conquered the Mamluk empire, and Turkish officials and soldiers filled Palestine. The local governor at Nablus was under the jurisdiction of Gaza, and the visibility of the Samaritan community in the capital increased with the rise in administrative traffic with Nablus. In the short run Jews (with whom the Ottomans included the Samaritans) prospered. In 1527 Suleiman the Magnificent, son of Selim, restored the walls of Jerusalem and reportedly gave Jews command of the gates. The sultan had a Jewish physician, and Jewish immigration to Egypt increased. In the long run, however, the Jews and inhabitants of Palestine in general had entered a period of decline. (Christians had already become a target of the Ottomans.) The Samaritan community withered as its leaders were imprisoned,[24] perhaps because they had sided with the Mamluks. Manuscript copying gradually declined, first in Gaza, then Egypt, and finally in Damascus.

Pinhas, the high priest at Nablus, spent a fifteen-year exile in Damascus (ca. 1523–1538) while a sizable Samaritan population still resided there. The officiating priest in Nablus during the absence of Pinhas was Hassebhi b.

---

[21] Strugnell, "Quelques inscriptions samaritaines," 555–80, esp. 577.
[22] Montgomery, *Samaritans,* 137.
[23] Alan Crown, "Samaritan Minuscule Paleography," *BJRL* 63 (1981): 344–47.
[24] Pummer, "Samaritan Material Remains and Archaeology," 228.

Joseph b. Abraham, who produced several manuscripts including von Gall's O and Gothic I, both copied for patrons in Egypt. Two scroll cases give us a glimpse of the Samaritan community in Damascus in this century: CW 2465 in the Chamberlain-Warren collection (crafted in 1524) and another from 1565.

The Chamberlain-Warren case is constructed of three equal curved sections bound together by hinges such that when closed the case completely encircles the scroll. It is 51 cm high with a 19 cm diameter, and is made of brass with inlaid silver design and an inscription. The case is shut with a bronze latch. The scroll case is a secondary use of the brass that forms it. Originally, the brass was fashioned into a large flat sheet, presumably a tray. Etched arabesque designs and Arabic religious phrases covered the tray. These etchings and inscriptions now appear on the interior surface of the scroll case. The apparent incongruity of having Islamic religious phrases on the case containing the most sacred object of the Samaritan community seems to have bothered no one.

The Benguiat case has the same structure as the Chamberlain-Warren case, although it has different dimensions—61 cm by 12.75 cm. The Benguiat case is brass with inlaid silver design and inscription. As with the Chamberlain-Warren case, each section of the Benguiat case includes one-third of a top and bottom end piece to complete the enclosure. Both pieces underwent secondary attachment to the barrel of the case by means of brass slotted screws (rather than rivets as with the latch and hinges). The repair work obscured some of the inscriptions along the bottom of the case.

Two handles proceed from the bottom of the case. A simple brass latch locks it. Each section of the case consists of panels separated by borders etched into the brass and outlined in silver. The inscriptions, again etched in silver, follow these borders. The panels themselves bear arabesque geometrical designs. These also are etched in silver, although now some of the silver has worn off.

Samaritan artisans have crafted several inscriptions onto the cases. On the Chamberlain-Warren case (CW 2465), the first appears midway down the barrel. The inscription consists of just three words, one on each of the case's three sections. The band on which the inscription appears divides each section of the case into two halves. The inscription reads:

יברכך יהוה וישמרך

Yahweh bless you and keep you.

This phrase quotes verbatim the priestly blessing in Numbers 6:24 as both the Masoretic Text and the Samaritan Pentateuch preserved it.

Benguiat scroll case. *Used by permission: Jewish Museum of New York.*

On the six borders formed by the ends of the case and the band of the first inscription traveling around it appears the following series of inscriptions.

ויהי בנסע
הארון ויאמר
משה קומה
יהוה ויפוצו
איביך וינוסו
משנאיך מפניך

As the ark departed, Moses said, "Arise Yahweh and scatter your enemies. The ones who hate you will flee from before you."

This quotation of Numbers 10:35 appears without variation from the Masoretic Text and von Gall's Samaritan Pentateuch except for the full spelling of the vowels of the hollow verbs ויפוצו and וינוסו which appear in both the Samaritan Pentateuch and the Masoretic Text as ויפצו and וינסו. Since the quotation on the scroll case probably conforms to the reading on the scroll inside itself, this full reading may provide one clue as to the spelling practices and even grammatical usage of the family of scrolls associated with the Chamberlain-Warren case.[25] This observation is striking, for von Gall lists no variant readings that match the rendition inscribed upon the case.

A dedicatory inscription also appears around the circumference of the top and bottom of the case. At the top it reads:

בשם יה עשה זה הארון למכתב
הקדוש בדמשק העבד המסכין בשיש
בוראי אלה אבי הפתח בן יוסף בן

In the name of Yah this case was made for the Holy Writing in Damascus (by) the miserable servant, the least of the creatures of God, Avi Hafatah son of Joseph son of . . .

Around the bottom of the case the inscription continues:

יעקב בן צפר דמבני מנשה יה יכפר
חטאתו אמן בשנת שלשים ותשע מאות
למלכות בני ישמעאל על יד יצחק ה . . .

Jacob son of Zophar of the family of Manasseh. May Yah forgive his sin. Amen. In the year 930 of the reign of the sons of Ishmael by the hand of Isaac . . .

The upper inscription notes that the case was made for the "holy writing in Damascus . . ." in order to contain the scroll, which predates it. The biblical quotations on the case presumably have the "holy writing in Damascus" as their source, which means that the case's biblical quotations reflect Damascene readings. Thus a full spelling with ו exists when a defective spelling

---

[25] See Robert Anderson, "Samaritan Pentateuch: General Account," in *The Samaritans* (ed. Alan Crown; Tübingen: Mohr, 1989), 393; and Terry Giles, "The Chamberlain-Warren Samaritan Inscription CW 2472," *JBL* 114 (1995): 111–16. This use of ו is typical of Samaritan orthography. See James Purvis, *The Samaritan Pentateuch and the Origin of the Samaritan Sect* (Cambridge: Harvard University Press, 1968), 68.

would be acceptable, and ו is absent in the dedicatory inscription (בשנת), when its presence would be expected. If the quotation were copied from an exemplar of the family of scrolls housed in the case, the alternative spelling in Numbers 10:35 would still provide evidence of a rendition of the verse that von Gall does not attest. This reading must have been current in 1524, the year of the case's construction.

The significance of the final ה following the name יצחק is unknown. Perhaps, it marks the beginning of a title of Isaac left uninscribed.

A final inscription appears on the lower half of one section of the case.

כתבו פינחס בן אלעזר

Written by Pinchus, son of Eleazar.

Spoer assumed that this Pinchus had prepared the inscriptions for their engraving onto the case.[26] However, since the dedicatory inscription credits Avi Hafatah with the construction of the case and Isaac with the preparation of the inscriptions, it may be that Pinchus, perhaps the same Pinchus who was high priest from 1508 to 1548 and who fled to Damascus in 1523, was the copyist who prepared the scroll first housed by this case. Possibly, the masculine pronominal ending appearing on כתבו refers to a ספר (masc.) or a מכתב (masc.)[27] (that is, the scroll) and not a כתבה (fem.) (the inscription).

The inscriptions on the Benguiat case resemble those on the Chamberlain-Warren case. This is not surprising since both come from Damascus within a span of forty-one years (Chamberlain-Warren from 1524 and Benguiat from 1565).

First, as on the Chamberlain-Warren case, an inscription circles the center of the Benguiat case, separated by a border from the designs on each panel above and below it. The inscription consists of three words, one on each section of the case:

יברכך יהוה וישמרך

Yahweh bless you and keep you.

The phrase, from Numbers 6:24, takes pride of place on each case.

---

[26] Hans Spoer, "Description of the Case of the Roll of a Samaritan Pentateuch," *JAOS* 27 (1906): 107.

[27] The translation of כתבה as "writing" is debatable. Abraham Cohen pointed out (oral communication) that at least one relevant tradition suggests that כתבה is better understood as "stylus" or "writing instrument." See *m. ʾAbot* 5:6.

The second inscription consists of six phrases written horizontally on each long side of the three segments of the case. Again, this inscription follows the pattern on the Chamberlain-Warren case, albeit with differences.

ויהי בנסע

הארון ויאמר

[מ]שה קומה

[יהוה ויפוצ]

] [יך ויינוסו

משנאיך מפניך

As the ark departed, [Mo]ses said, "Arise Yahweh and scatter your [enemies]. The ones who hate you will flee from before you."

This quotation from Numbers 10:35 preserves the full spelling of ויפוצ and ויינוסו as does the Chamberlain-Warren case, in opposition to all other manuscripts listed by von Gall. Apparently, the cases' makers copied the biblical texts from the same manuscript family, if not the same scroll. Obviously, this one orthographic peculiarity does not provide sufficient evidence for determining a text type. But according to the principle of internal consistency identified by Judith Sanderson[28] in her work on 4QpaleoExod^m, this rendition of Numbers 10:35 may provide a clue to the character of the scroll behind the inscriptions. Inscriptions on the case thus provide evidence not only for the family of the manuscript housed in the case but also for the scroll's date, provenance, and producers, in short a traceable history of the manuscript and its family.

Additional inscriptions appear on the six panels formed by the upper and lower halves of each section of the case. The six inscriptions note:

יהוה שמו יהוה נסי

Yahweh is his name, Yahweh My Banner.
(Exod 17:15)

יהוה אל רחום יחנון

Yahweh God merciful and gracious.
(Exod 34:6)

אלהיך יראה יהוה יראה

Your God will provide; Yahweh will provide.
(Gen 22:8,14)

---

[28] Judith Sanderson, *An Exodus Scroll from Qumran: 4QpaleoExod^m and the Samaritan Tradition* (Atlanta: Scholars Press, 1986), 313.

יהוה אלהי יהוה גבור

Yahweh is my God; Yahweh is mighty.
(Exod 15:11,3?)

יהוה אלהינו יהוה אחד

Yahweh is our God; Yahweh is one.
(Deut 6:4)

על יד הרבן **אביעזי** בן הרבן יוסף בדמשך

By the hand of Rabban Abiazi, son of Rabban Joseph in Damascus.

Finally, a dedicatory inscription circles both the top and the bottom of the barrel of the case. Around the top, it reads:

בשם יה עשה זה הארון למכ[ ]
הק[ ] בד [ ] העבד הנשש יוסף
בן **אבזפוה** דמבני פתר

In the name of Yah this case was made for the ho[ly]
w[riting] in Da[mascus] by the humble servant Joseph
son of Abizophoh of the family of Patar.

At the bottom it continues:

בשנת הועוחק לממ[ ]
בני יש׃ יה׃ יכפר לת חטע
אמן רעת בהישמע תלה רם חי

In the year 976 of the rule of
the sons of Ish[mael]. May Yah forgive him his sin.
Amen. Mischief while hearing hangs (i.e., chokes) abundant life.[29]

The ב prepositional prefix followed by a nonelided ה signifying the definite article in the word בהישמע of line three is rare but not unknown in Samaritan inscriptions,[30] and may reflect a northern Israelite spelling practice.[31]

---

[29] This last line is not mentioned in the description of the case offered by Adler and Casanowicz. The line seems to mean: "Lack of attention or a neglect of attention (presumably to the reading of Torah) will lead to the end of abundant life."

[30] Giles, "Chamberlain-Warren Samaritan Inscriptions," 114–15.

[31] Gary Rendsburg, *Linguistic Evidence for the Northern Origin of Selected Psalms* (Atlanta: Scholars Press, 1990), 40.

A final inscription, in a different hand, is scratched along the edge of one of the sections making up the barrel of the case. It seems to postdate the construction of the case, for its execution is crude, it interrupts the symmetry of the inscriptions, and it was never embossed with silver. Unlike any of the other inscriptions on the case, it also employs dots as word dividers. It is impossible to date this inscription or offer a reason for its existence. Perhaps a worshiper sought to commemorate the reading of Torah by leaving his mark upon the scroll case in the form of graffiti. The scratched inscription reads as follows:

עמר עתיק יעמר

The house (in which) the Torah will dwell.

עתיק ("ancient") sometimes serves as a metaphor for "Torah." In Middle Aramaic, עמר is a noun, the verb form of which means "to dwell." The inscription thus forms a well-balanced and pious expression of respect for the scroll "house."

To summarize, these two scroll cases preserve, by means of decorative inscriptions etched into each, valuable evidence for the family of scrolls formerly within them. Both originating in Damascus, the cases date to within four decades of each other. The inscriptions on the cases are remarkable in that they agree in their rendition of Numbers 10:35 against all of the other known witnesses listed by von Gall. This agreement cannot simply be a reflex of a scribal convention of sixteenth-century Damascus. Although now empty, these cases stand as vibrant witness to one strand within the recension of the Samaritan Pentateuch.

Damascus continued to foster meetings between Samaritans and other religious groups. While the homogeneous Nablus community championed undiluted Samaritan traditions, contacts with other faiths in Damascus modified the sect's beliefs and literature. For example, during this period, the Damascene Jewish community grew and prospered with the influx of refugees from Spain including R. Jacob Berab and a number of other scholars and kabbalists. Their influence is evident in the second Samaritan list of the 613 precepts found in Sayr al-Qalb that the Damascene Samaritan Abraham ha-Qabasi wrote in 1532.[32] When Pinhas and his son Eleazar returned to Nablus, Abraham ha-Qabasi and Sedaqah b. Jacob of the Munis family, known to us as a witness in several manuscript transactions, moved with them to Shechem.

---

[32] Menahem Haran, "The Song of the Precepts of Aaron ben Manir," *PIASH* 5 (1974), 1–36.

The poverty of the Samaritan community during this period was reflected in manuscript prices, which declined at a rate exceeding two percent
per year, a trend that reversed toward the end of the century, when political
conditions became more stable. The market for liturgical works increased,
and Europeans began to buy manuscripts.[33]

The Samaritan community itself continued its decline. In 1544 Istakhri
wrote (on the authority of Jews in Jerusalem) that "Nablus is the city of the
Samaritans, and they possess no other city on the face of the earth."[34] In
1574 Murad III began his reign by ordering the execution of all Jews. Although the state rescinded the order, Jews were required to sport small turbans and not wear silk.[35] By the end of the century an English visitor
described Jerusalem as a ruin, and a twentieth-century encyclopedia article
blithely states that "on the whole Palestine ceases from this point to have a
history till the coming of the nineteenth century."[36] Awareness of the Samaritan past, however, grows among historians outside the group.

---

[33] Crown, "Manuscript Prices," 92–93.
[34] Montgomery, *Samaritans,* 135.
[35] DeHaas, *History of Palestine,* 338.
[36] Robert Macalister, "Palestine: IV. From the Turkish Conquest to 1918," *Encyclopaedia Britannica* (1953) 17:131–32.

Chapter 7

The Modern Period

The sixteenth century, paradoxically, witnessed both the continuous decline of the Samaritans and the birth of Samaritan studies in Europe. The invasion of the Ottoman Turks early in the sixteenth century led to greater
oppression of the Samaritans, provoking many to return to Nablus. One of
the treasures reaching there was the *Sayr al Qalb,* which Abraham ha-Qabasi
had written in Damascus. Within a century, the Samaritan community at
Damascus had disappeared, and the demise of the Egyptian community was
not far behind.

Persecution of non-Muslims continued throughout the century, although the Samaritans seem to have suffered disproportionately. Samaritans
and Jews received different treatment, and again their respective political decisions were the cause. As in the past, when Samaritans and Jews were torn
between supporting various dominant powers—Persia or Greece, Greece or
Rome, Rome or Byzantia, Byzantia or Islam—they now again had to choose
between Turk and Arab, and this time the Jews made the better choice when
they chose the Turks, the ultimate winners. In consequence, Nablus was partially destroyed, and Jews settled there.

Turkish tax records provide partial census numbers for the Samaritans.

NABLUS		1538/9	1548/9		1596/7
Heads of households		29	34		20
Bachelors		4	1		

GAZA	1525/6	1538/9	1548/9	1556/7	1596/7
Heads of households	25	15	18	18	8
Bachelors		2			

Schur uses the formula of four to a family to estimate a total of 220 Samaritans in Palestine in 1538.[1] Adding the populations of Egypt (ca. 200)
and Damascus (ca. 100) would yield a population in the mid-sixteenth century that was approximately what it is today.

[1] Schur, *History of the Samaritans,* 123.

SAMARITAN MANUSCRIPTS ARRIVE IN THE WEST

Early in the Ottoman period European scholars became aware of the Samaritans and their literature. Diplomacy between the Ottomans and the French began at least as early as 1531 when Francis I began to encourage the sultan to invade Italy, and was in evidence again in 1543 when Suleiman's fleet wintered in Toulon. Political events in the Middle East focused scholarly attention in that direction as well. In 1537 Guillaume Postel acquired a Samaritan grammar and included comments on it and the Samaritans themselves in his work, *Le traité des douze langues,* the following year. It was the first information published in a Western language on the Samaritans since Jerome's prologue to the *Book of Kings* back in the fourth century. Sometime late in the sixteenth century Joseph Scaliger, a self-taught Semitist, began a correspondence with the Samaritan communities at Nablus and Egypt in an attempt to secure a copy of their Pentateuch. In 1584 he did receive some materials including a copy of the Samaritan *Joshua* that Abd-el Ghani had written in 1362–1363 (published by Juynboll in 1848 and later by O. T. Crane in 1890). This initiated a long-term, multifaceted correspondence between Samaritans and European scholars. He also received letters, some posthumously, but no copy of the Pentateuch. The Samaritans may have been reluctant to entrust their sacred text to outsiders, although some speculate that they were holding out for money, or that perhaps a text was sent but lost at sea.

In 1590 two letters, one from Gaza and the other from Egypt, reached the already deceased Scaliger in response to questions he had raised. They ended up in the hands of Nicholas Fabri de Peiresc, an inveterate bibliophile who traveled extensively in the Middle East and Europe. He in turn passed them on to Jean Morin, a scholar at the Oratory in Paris who published a Latin translation of the letters. In 1783 Johann Gottfried Eichhorn republished them with text and translation in volume 13 of his *Repertorium.*[2]

In the seventeenth century Western travelers began to describe their journeys through Samaritan communities. The French ambassador to Istanbul, Francois de Breves, visited Gaza in 1604, and his secretary met Samaritans in Ramleh. A companion of de Breves, Henry de Beauveau, left behind provocative comments on the Gaza Samaritans' religious practices, dress, and funerary practices:

> They do not eat entire fruit, nor food which has been prepared artificially, nor hybrid mixtures. At Passover they roast a calf and they cover their bodies and

---

[2] Johann Gottfried Eichhorn, *Repertorium für biblische und morgenländische Literatur* (Leipzig, 1783), volume 13, beginning at page 277.

wash themselves with ash from this calf. This they do in order to atone for their sins.

The Samaritans who are about to die, lie outside, without a roof, so that their souls can ascend to heaven. They do not touch their dead, and others bury them. They do not eat food which has been touched by those of another persuasion, and if one of the coreligionists has eaten a piece of meat in secret, they throw away the rest of the meat, as if it were unclean. As to their clothing, they wear them only after they have been placed in a well closed box, which cannot be penetrated, and the box is then immersed seven times in water. Someone told us that they place also a pigeon in the box, so as to adore it, and they say that the pigeon is the one from the ark of Noah.

Otherwise they are quite prudent people and very rich, they do not deal in any trade nor in other matters in Gaza, except for serving as clerks to the pasha and to other people.[3]

The most consequential visitor of the seventeenth century was the Italian Pietro della Valle, who visited each of the major centers, Cairo, Gaza, Nablus, and Damascus, and in the last city purchased the first Samaritan Pentateuch to reach Europe. He also made several notations regarding the Samaritans.

Robert Huntington visited Nablus in 1671 looking for Samaritan manuscripts and soon initiated a correspondence with the community. Henry Maundrell, an English clergyman, had a conversation with the Samaritan high priest in Nablus in 1697. A year later the French canon Antoine Morison met with a Samaritan family in Nablus, offering a glimpse of the large families some members of the sect had.[4] His lack of mention of sacrifices on Mount Gerizim may indicate that the ban on them by Mehmed IV a few decades earlier was still in effect.

Pietro della Valle (1586–1652) was a poet, orator, and soldier for the papacy who was born and died in Rome. He traveled extensively in the Middle East and ventured as far as India, where he stayed for two years. He tells many strange tales about his travels, including keeping the body of his deceased wife with him for a portion of his journey.

The opportunity for Westerners to study the Samaritan Pentateuch had to await the early seventeenth century, when Pietro della Valle did find a copy

---

[3] Henri de Beauveau, *Relation journalière du voyage du Levant* (Toul, 1608), 144–46; cited in Schur, *History of the Samaritans,* 126–27.

[4] Montgomery, *Samaritans,* 114.

(von Gall's codex B, dated 1345–1346) in Damascus. The sale of a copy of their Pentateuch derived from the growing impoverishment of the community in Damascus in the seventeenth century. The seventeenth-century Damascene Samaritan community suffered from the Muslims and died out within fifteen years of the purchase. The manuscript, meanwhile, arrived in Paris in 1623, where Jean Morin studied and published it.

While pursuing his studies of philosophy, theology, math, Greek, Latin, and Hebrew, Morin became disenchanted with his Protestantism. He converted to Roman Catholicism and became a scholar at the Oratory in Paris. The arrival of the della Valle manuscript in Morin's hands marked a watershed in textual criticism. He remained at the center of all discussion of the Samaritan Pentateuch for three decades, from the arrival of the della Valle codex, through its publication in the Paris polyglot of 1645, until the incomplete catalogue of Samaritan texts that he published in 1657. Meanwhile, an incomplete and composite pentateuchal manuscript (von Gall's K) had somehow made its way to Italy in 1621, but either because of its poor quality or the lack of expertise in Italy, it elicited no study.

After the publication of the Walton or London polyglot of 1657, a flurry of interest in the Samaritan Pentateuch prompted the sending of emissaries to the Middle East in search of more copies. Because the Samaritan text seemed to support the Roman Catholic-favored Septuagint against the Masoretic Text that Jews and Protestants considered the original text, the issue became important in polemics between Roman Catholics and Protestants. This interest may have prevented any thorough, systematic examination and comparison of the texts.

In any case, within a year of Codex B's arrival in Paris, others began to appear in the British Isles, solicited mainly by Archbishop Ussher in his quest for accurate dating of biblical events. He received six pentateuchal manuscripts during the next decade, of which von Gall's N, dated 1362–1363, is the most easily identifiable.

The French collection of pentateuchal manuscripts likewise grew with the aid of Nicholas Peiresc, who in 1628 acquired von Gall's C, including a leaf from another pentateuchal manuscript in both Hebrew and Arabic, and von Gall's M, a triglot composed of the text in Aramaic, Arabic, and Hebrew. Peiresc took an unrivaled interest in the Arabic pentateuchal manuscripts and successfully imported at least two to France, one in 1633, the other in 1684.

SAMARITAN CORRESPONDENCE WITH THE WEST

European interest in their community and writings puzzled the Samaritans, who concluded that members of the sect must be living in Europe, particularly in England, where Ussher's solicitation was pronounced. A few Englishmen encouraged this delusion as a strategy for obtaining more Samaritan writings and as a tool for proselytizing. They had the precedent of della Valle, who contrived to get copies of the Samaritan holy books "in any way possible: by purchase, or by some trick."[5]

Among the opportunists was the aforementioned Robert Huntington, who, after a gap of almost a century, reestablished European contact with Samaritans. He visited Nablus in 1671 while serving as chaplain to an English community at Aleppo. The Samaritans were as intrigued with him as he was with them. They especially appreciated his ability to read their script and inquired if there were "Israelites" in England. When Huntington answered in the affirmative, they assumed that Samaritans lived in England. Huntington decided to exploit their confusion rather than correct it. Initially the ruse paid off. He received at least one copy of the Pentateuch (von Gall's Gothic A, currently in the Bodleian Library at Oxford, where it is numbered as Marsh 15 after the archbishop to whom Huntington presented it). It was the final Samaritan Pentateuch to arrive in Europe in the seventeenth century.

Huntington received a letter at Jerusalem in 1672 that the Samaritans wished to have delivered to their "brothers" in England.[6] The letter describes the religious practices of the community at Nablus, requests a copy of the "English Samaritan" Torah in return for the one they had already sent to England, and requests that a wise and able priest of the lineage of Pinhas come to them, presumably to reinstate the failed priesthood at Nablus. (Samaritans have attached particular importance to the priest Pinhas, the grandson of Aaron. Since the Taheb, or Messiah, should descend from his line, it was urgent that the line continue. In practice the priesthood devolved upon the Levitical family.)

In 1675, the Samaritans sent a second letter, written in Hebrew using the Samaritan characters, from Gaza to their coreligionists in England. The scribe was Marhib/Mufarrij b. Jacob b. Joseph of Nablus, who had written other letters as well. This letter described various rituals at Nablus and requested that the English Samaritans describe themselves. Meanwhile, the first letter had reached Thomas Marshall at Oxford, who intentionally misled the Samaritans, partly to obtain manuscripts from them and partly to proselytize them. He responded in Hebrew to their letter, claiming to be of the "tribe of Japheth" and pretending to speak on behalf of a sizable Samaritan

[5] Schur, *History of the Samaritans,* 129.
[6] Sylvester de Sacy, "Correspondance des Samaritains de Naplouse," *Notices et Extraits des Manuscrits de la Bibliotheque du Roi* 12 (1831): 162–74.

community that owned a copy of the *Sepher Joshua* older than any in Nablus, as well as many other books of psalms, liturgy, and prophets. He raised questions with them apparently to push them in the direction of Christianity. He asked them who will be the great prophet, who is the star that must depart from Jacob, and who is Hashilo or Soliman. Huntington brought this letter and one of his own to the Samaritans. In his own letter, Huntington baited the Samaritans with the ancient Jewish accusation that they worshiped a dove on Mount Gerizim. This letter appears only in T. Smith's *R. Huntingtoni Epistolae* of 1704.

The Samaritans resented the accusation and responded within the year in a package of three letters, one in Arabic addressed to Huntington, and similar ones in Arabic and Hebrew addressing their English fellow believers. Each letter has a testy overtone. In their letter to Huntington they express surprise that he would refer again to the dove cult accusation. They take Marshall to task because he did not identify himself or any of the Samaritans in England. They acknowledge his request for a copy of the *Sepher Joshua* but challenge him to send them a copy of his first. To facilitate more communication, they describe some of their religious practices. Another letter in Arabic for the nonexistent English Samaritans at Oxford was communicated through Huntington in 1688.[7]

Meanwhile a new line of correspondence opened between the Samaritans and Europe when Job Ludolf, an Amsterdam scholar, wrote a letter to the sect in 1684 with the help of a Jewish acquaintance who had informed him of them. The next year they responded to his questions in two missives, written in Samaritan Hebrew, discussing among other things the concept of the messiah, a favorite issue among the Europeans. The Samaritans informed Ludolf that the messiah has not yet come. A third letter, also in Samaritan Hebrew, reached Ludolf in 1691 (dated 1689) after he had responded to the first two.[8]

French scholars were also misleading the Samaritans as a means of procuring more of their documents (although, in their defense, there is some indication of a Samaritan presence in France). Two Arabic Samaritan Pentateuchs from 1685 bear notes from their respective scribes, the prolific Salamah b. Jacob b. Murjan b. Abraham b. Ishmael of the Danfi family for CW 10262 and Yuhanna ibn Girgis ibn Qatta for Arabe 3. Each includes reproductions of the notes from their sources, and it is clear that both scribes copied from a text bearing a colophon claiming that the manuscript of which it was a part was brought to Paris by Capuchin "rabbis" in 1684. Either some

---

[7] De Sacy, "Correspondance des Samaritains," 220–22.
[8] De Sacy, "Correspondance des Samaritains," 11–12.

Samaritans resided in Paris, or this claim was a ruse—complicating the problem is the fact that one of the 1685 manuscripts surfaced in Palestine at the turn of the twentieth century.

The volume of correspondence during the seventeenth century and its general tone suggest that the Samaritans generally lived free from oppression and poverty, a picture that at least one European traveler who visited the community confirms.[9]

Abraham al-'Ayya of the Danfi family initiated a Samaritan renaissance in the eighteenth century. His position as secretary to the Turkish governor of the district of Nablus enabled him to give considerable political aid to the community. He arranged for the return of the high priest Tabia b. Isaac from exile in Gaza, and he was able to purchase land on Mount Gerizim. With his uncle Meshalmah b. Murjan (owner of one of manuscripts in the Chamberlain-Warren collection), he wrote a commentary on the Pentateuch (except Deuteronomy). Ghazal b. Abu'l Sarur b. Ghazal also produced several religious works during this period. The Samaritan community resided exclusively at Nablus after the last vestiges of a diaspora at Jaffa and Gaza perished during Napoleon's invasion of the Levant in 1799.

Few letters between Samaritans and Europeans break the general silence of the eighteenth century. One is an undated letter from Meshalmah b. Ab Sakhwah (presumably b. Abraham of the Danfi family in Nablus, the scribe of Rylands 2 and Gaster 820; he was active between 1707 and 1739 and is the only person by that name for whom any record exists). The letter notes the demise of the high-priestly lineage and appeals to European coreligionists to send them good, wise, men of the priestly line of Pinhas. In 1790 a letter from the Samaritans addressed the brethren in France. It later surfaced in Holland and was published in 1834 by A. A. Hamaker.

Early in the nineteenth century, Henri Gregoire, Bishop of Blois, with the assistance of Silvestre de Sacy, initiated a significant correspondence between the Samaritans and Europeans. M. Corancoz composed the introductory letter in 1808, posing a series of thirty questions developed by the French scholars. They were particularly intrigued by possible links between the Samaritans and Karaites, an antirabbinical sect of Judaism that emerged late in the first millennium C.E. Both groups used complex calendars that required specialists to establish feast days for a given year, and even the formula for calculating some feasts, notably Pentecost, differed from that of orthodox Judaism. In response to direct questioning the Samaritans affirmed their distinctiveness.[10] Many of the practices they share with Karaism can be traced

---

[9] Schur, *History of the Samaritans,* 127.
[10] De Sacy, "Correspondance des Samaritains," 52–63.

back to Zadokite traditions at Qumran and may help establish the family tree of a particular form of Judaism.

The Karaites, like the Jews and the Samaritans, are another surviving sect in modern Israel that base their identity on the Hebrew Scriptures. Their antirabbinical stand led European scholars in the nineteenth century to look for links between them and the Samaritans. Both had developed complex calendars that required the priests to establish the dates of the feast days and both ignored postbiblical Jewish commentaries on Scripture. They shared practices traceable back to traditions described in the Dead Sea Scrolls. Modern Karaites and Samaritans are unaware of any relationship between their two groups in either the past or the present.

The Europeans were interested in other issues as well: the location and number of the Samaritan communities, their distinctive rituals, and most provocatively their alleged worship of the dove. The Samaritans answered matter-of-factly, acknowledging the decline of the communities and the demise of the Aaronic line of priesthood, and describing the religious and practical origins of many of their rituals. They also strongly asserted their distinctiveness and again repudiated the dove cult.[11] That correspondence was the major source for Samaritan studies until the end of the century.

In his letter, Corancoz asked for a copy of the Samaritan calendar of festivals "to give to the Samaritans in France." This ruse, along with earlier deceptions by Huntington and Marshall, encouraged the Samaritans to believe that there were compatriots in Europe. De Sacy commented:

> You can see by what is written here that the author of the letter to which Salemeh responds allows many untrue assertions that would not in the least inspire the confidence of simple people, who, already fooled many times by similar allegations, must regard as impostors all Europeans who look to establish relationships with them today.[12]

The letter evoked sixteen further questions from de Sacy and the bishop, which they communicated to the Samaritans in 1810. In the middle of the next year, they received a long reply in Hebrew and a shorter one in Arabic. These missives describe the manner of the sect's sacrifices, outline their language, and again deny the dove worship. In 1820 de Sacy received a letter in Arabic accompanied by a table of contemporary astronomical observations and a Hebrew letter addressing the brethren in Europe, again begging them

---

[11] De Sacy, "Correspondance des Samaritains," 52–63.
[12] De Sacy, "Correspondance des Samaritains," 150. Translation ours.

for some response. In his letter to de Sacy, the scribe, Salamah b. Tabiah b. Isaac b. Abraham b. Isaac b. Sadaqah, an active scribe between 1783 and 1848, responds to several questions regarding the burial of the dead, the resurrection, and the images on the scroll case containing the Pentateuch. De Sacy denies writing the letter and expresses surprise that the Samaritans know his name.

The Samaritans persisted in their attempt to contact their European brethren. In 1826 those in Palestine wrote a letter in Hebrew to the Samaritans in Paris inquiring into their prayers and practices. England and France were the two countries where the Samaritans assumed their brethren were located. The initial confusion in England probably resulted from misunderstanding Jews as Israelites and thus Samaritans. As already described, the confusion served the purposes of both English and French scholars.

In the first half of the nineteenth century many Samaritans died in a series of campaigns by Ottoman forces determined to bring the anarchic district of Nablus under firm control. In 1831 Ibrahim of Egypt successfully invaded Syria and Palestine, captured Nablus, and offered temporary relief to the Samaritans. They experienced new religious freedom, including access to Mount Gerizim, and the Passover celebration on the mountain recommenced. But Egypt held control for only a decade. The Turks soon reclaimed the region and revenged themselves on the Samaritans. The Samaritans, threatened by a group of fanatical Muslims committed to ethnic cleansing, addressed a plaintive petition to the government of Louis Philippe.[13] The Muslims relented in exchange for a large payment of money from the Samaritan community and the Jewish chief rabbi in Jerusalem, who assured them that the Samaritans were also a "people of the Book."

Another letter from the Samaritans addressed to a European government, this time that of Great Britain, arrived in 1875. It is now in the British Museum (Or. 1381).

The Samaritans also survived the hostilities of Turkish leaders extorting large sums of money from them in the mid- to late nineteenth century. Their most helpful survival strategy was to seek security from the British consul. However, this habit alienated the Muslims, costing the Samaritans government jobs, although it did insure the community's survival into the twentieth century.

E. Kautzsch obtained and published an 1884 letter from the Samaritan high priest, Jacob ibn Harun (apparently Aaron).[14] It contains answers to

---

[13] Jean Joseph L. Barges, *Les Samaritains de Naplouse: Épisode d'une pèlerinage dans les lieux saints* (Paris: Dondey-Dupre, 1855), 81.

[14] E. Kautzsch, "Ein Brief des Hohenpriesters der Samaritaner Ja'kub ibn Harun," *ZDPV* 8 (1885).

questions concerning the numbers of their community, their internal legal arrangements, and the Taheb. The last exchange of letters in the nineteenth century was between Jacob ben Aaron and J. Rosenberg, focused on a discussion of a copy of *Sepher Hayamim* that the Samaritans owned. In 1901 Rosenberg published *Lehrbuch der samaritanischen Sprache und Literatur* at Leipzig describing the correspondence.

> Moses Gaster fled persecution in Rumania, his homeland, in 1885 and settled in England, where he became the Chief Rabbi of the British Sephardic Jews. He had an interest in many aspects of Semitic culture and published widely. He had a longstanding relationship with the Samaritan community at Nablus and visited them when he could. They helped him accumulate a large collection of manuscripts and census data, often making copies of manuscripts that were otherwise unavailable to him.

During the early part of the twentieth century, an extensive correspondence was carried on between the Samaritans and Moses Gaster. A man of many interests, Gaster showed a special concern for the community after he visited them during travels in Palestine in 1906. He was intent upon obtaining copies of all their works and did a remarkable job of soliciting, buying, and commissioning manuscripts, as the collection in the John Rylands Library at the University of Manchester attests. He visited the Samaritans in Nablus, and at least two Samaritan priests visited him in London.

> Jacob, the long-time high priest, in 1902 sent a letter to the Boys School in Jerusalem protesting the activities of the priest Isaac Cohen. Isaac was in London, purporting to be the head of the Samaritan Community and soliciting money for Samaritan charities. His visit had been written up in a London paper, and Jacob wanted to clarify that the visit was not sanctioned by the Samaritan community. The letter and a cover letter were referred to Dr. Adler of the Alliance Israelite Universalle in Paris, who in turn forwarded them along with his own cover letter to Moses Gaster. All three letters are in the Samaritan collection of the John Rylands Library at Manchester.

Gaster continued his contact with the Samaritan community through a very extensive correspondence, a representative selection of which Edward Robertson describes. Given Gaster's interest in the study of Samaritan documents, it is not surprising that much of the correspondence concerns the availability and purchase of manuscripts. At least three letters focus on the acquisition of a copy of the Samaritan *Book of Joshua*. Gaster had already received several copies of the book in 1906 and considered its discovery one of his significant accomplishments. Despite the controversy that his evaluation of the work provoked, or perhaps because of it, Gaster continued to pursue more and older copies. On February 8, 1908, he wrote to Aaron b. Pinhas, the priest, soliciting his help in finding an ancient copy of the book (Item 352 in Robertson's *Catalogue*).[15] Aaron responded on at least one occasion (Item 366 in Robertson) and Ab Hasda on another (Item 347), each reporting his failure to locate any ancient copies of the book. Ab Hasda, Abraham, and Abisha b. Pinhas all sent letters offering other manuscripts for sale (Items 347, 357, 358, 359, 363, 364, 366). The most interesting one was the fiftieth Torah copied by Abi Berakhatah b. Ab Zehuta b. Ab Nefusha b. Abraham, and the *tashqil* appears in the letter.

Two letters from Ab Hasda respond to Gaster's inquiries about the Abisha scroll (Items 358 and 347). The first includes the *tashqil;* the second offers a detailed description of the scroll's materials, measurements, and coloring. In this letter Ab Hasda states that the only photographs of the Abisha scroll are those that the American Samaritan Committee had taken at a cost of twenty pounds. The latter committee was chaired by the aforementioned E. K. Warren (see Chapter One), and included as its most prominent member William E. Barton, an American clergyman, who published several articles on the Samaritans and aided in the editing and publishing of works by the high priest, Jacob. The committee persuaded the Samaritans to allow the Abisha scroll to be photographed in hopes that this would help them become financially self-sufficient.

At least two letters respond to questions that Gaster raised (e.g., in Robertson, Item 362) about Samaritan beliefs and practices. Both responses (Items 348 and 365) cite Abisha and describe ablutions, other ceremonies, and the Samaritan position on sorcery. Some letters focus on personal matters: complaints about Gaster's failure to respond (Items 354, 356, 359, and 367), a request for his help in recovering payment for five manuscripts sent to a man in Milwaukee (Item 358), and a letter denouncing a fellow Samaritan, Isaac b. Amram, who was in London purporting to be a high priest representing the Samaritan community (Item 346. 1–3). In the last case, Jacob asks Gaster to repudiate the article about Isaac that has appeared in a London newspaper. Actually Gaster seems to have appreciated Isaac's visit and to have gained from it both information and manuscripts.[16]

---

[15] Edward Robertson, *Catalogue of the Samaritan Manuscripts in the John Rylands Library Manchester* (2 vols.; Manchester: John Rylands Library, 1962), 2:265.

[16] Moses Gaster, *Studies and Texts in Folklore, Magic, Mediaeval Romance, Hebrew Apocrypha, and Samaritan Archaeology* (3 vols.; London: Maggs, 1925–1928; repr., New York: Ktav, 1971), 1:614.

The last substantial collection of Samaritan letters addressed William E. Barton and E. K. Warren. This extensive correspondence presently resides at Boston University. The high priest Jacob b. Aaron b. Salamah wrote most of these letters in Arabic between 1903 and 1913. They were translated or dictated and written directly in English (a few are in French or German) by Dr. Gaskoin Wright or the Reverend S. Webb of the Missionary Hospital in Nablus. The collection includes the original Arabic texts as well as translations. In the initial letter of 1903, Jacob assured Barton that scribes had already written three chapters missing from a copy of Genesis that he had apparently commissioned. In response to a Barton query, Jacob also states that the "Christ" is still to come. Much of the correspondence deals with such theological and business questions.

When Jacob died in 1916, his son Abu'l Hassan continued the communications and the first post-World War I letters reveal a series of continuing concerns. Three letters arrived in 1918. Two were letters from Abu'l Hassan, one each to Warren and Barton; the third, addressed to Warren, was signed by a committee that included Abu'l Hassan.[17] All three described the wartime sufferings of the Samaritans, complained about the distribution of funds by the American Samaritan Committee, solicited money for the impoverished community, and expressed openness to answering questions. Abu'l Hassan, in his letter to Barton, laments the continued annual payments of twenty gold liras on a Pentateuch (CW 2481) he has pawned for ten Ottoman bank notes (about fifteen hundred francs or three hundred dollars) and asks for reimbursement. The letter from the committee acknowledges Warren's request to have the Abisha scroll photographed, a task that was subsequently accomplished, and also admits that the Samaritans often displayed for outsiders a second Pentateuch instead of the Abisha scroll.

Barton, apparently aware of the tension in the Samaritan community over the selection of a priest to succeed Jacob, asked both Abu'l Hassan and his competitor Isaac how a new high priest was selected. Both responded in letters dated in May, 1919. Isaac insists that he alone fits the criteria.

By the third decade of the twentieth century, the Samaritans had many legitimate reasons to be embittered against their Western friends. Warren, their great benefactor, had died. Many of their literary treasures that he had hoped to preserve in Nablus remained in Three Oaks, Michigan, as part of his estate. The Americans associated with Warren or handling affairs in Palestine were either less interested or were financially unable to help. With anger on one side and disinterest on the other, all communication soon ceased.

---

[17] W. E. Barton, "The War and the Samaritan Colony," *BSac* 78 (January 1921): 6–16.

During the nineteenth century the government denied Samaritans access to their sacred mountain, and the community's literary efforts had long since dwindled. In the early twentieth century their total population numbered fewer than two hundred. By the early twenty-first century that number has more than doubled, with the community equally divided between Nablus and Holon, a suburb of Tel Aviv.

In the latter part of the twentieth century an extensive relationship between the Europeans and Americans and the Samaritans opened, mainly through the participation of the Samaritan journalist Binyamim Sedaqa in several conferences of scholars studying the group, held in Europe and Israel, and his willingness to share material with these scholars. In the publication of the 1985 round table "Samaritan Manuscripts: Problems and Methods" held in Paris, Sedaqa comments:

> As these manuscripts spread around the world, from White Russia to the English libraries, from the Public Library in New York to the library of the University of Michigan [*sic*—Michigan State University] in the United States, and in spite of the fact that the Samaritans themselves never left Eretz Israel, these manuscripts represented the Samaritans as ambassadors around the world giving evidence to their existence. This stimulated the interest of influential people and researchers around the world in the fate of the Samaritans. . . . As there came to be a rising interest in the Samaritan manuscripts which were being taken from library shelves and dusted off.[18]

Historical tensions between rabbinic Judaism and Samaritanism remain minimal. Both are heirs of traditions and festivals authorized in the Pentateuch. Samaritans were legally Jews during much of the history of occupation in Palestine, and often the two groups recognized each other's authorities. Yet Samaritans do not consider themselves Jews, and this distinction informs both religious and social practices. They do not celebrate Purim, Hanukkah, or the four minor feasts that are rooted elsewhere in Jewish tradition. They are also reluctant to marry Jews, although, as a modern expediency, Samaritan men may marry Jewish women. For their part, Jews still have reservations about Samaritans and will not allow them to bury their dead in the Jewish cemetery at Tel Aviv.

---

[18] Jean-Pierre Rothschild and Guy Dominique Sixdennier, eds., *Étude samaritaines Pentateuque et Targum, exégèse et philologie, chroniques* (Louvain-Paris: Peeters, 1988), 291–92

Chapter 8

The Samaritan Pentateuch

Several of the Greek church fathers referred to the Samaritan Pentateuch. Origen (ca. 185–254) used a Greek translation of it, the *Samareitikon,* in notes in his *Hexapla,* and citations also feature in the works of Eusebius of Caesarea (263–339), Epiphanius (315–403), and Cyril of Jerusalem (315–386). Jerome (347–419) made use of it in his Latin translation of the Vulgate, and the Talmud reflects awareness of it, if only in a generally critical sense. However, more than a millennium passed before Western scholars cited the Samaritan Pentateuch again.

It is not clear when Europeans first became aware again of the Samaritan Pentateuch or what they anticipated would be its character, but a renaissance of Hebrew and Greek studies in the sixteenth century had inspired extensive research on the Vulgate (Latin), Septuagint (Greek), and Masoretic Hebrew texts. As already noted, Joseph Scaliger, a self-taught Semitist of the time became aware of the Samaritan Pentateuch and contacted the Samaritan community in hopes, vain as it turned out, of receiving a copy.

Some Anglicans feared that the Samaritan Pentateuch would challenge the readings of their preferred Masoretic Text. In a letter to Archbishop Ussher, William Eyres already argued for the authenticity of the Masoretic Text against either the Septuagint or the Samaritan Pentateuch, and this was fifteen years before he could have seen the latter! Ralph Skynner also alerted the archbishop to Roman Catholic claims that Moses gave each of the twelve tribes a copy of the Torah in Samaritan characters.

Eyres and Skynner correctly anticipated the polemical preoccupation of scholars when the first Samaritan Pentateuch, a 1345–1346 C.E. text acquired by della Valle, arrived in Europe. To be sure, the first salvo in the battle was muted, a brief description of the text (von Gall's B) in the preface of Morinus's 1628 work on the Septuagint. Morinus noted that the Samaritan Pentateuch seemed to support the Greek versions against the Masoretic Text.

Three years later, Morinus published a much fuller treatment of the Samaritan Pentateuch, triggering a controversy that lasted more than twenty-five years. The initial responses were mild. In June 1632 Archbishop Ussher in Ireland referred to Morinus's work in a letter to Ludovico Capellus of the Reformed Saumere Seminary, but his own interest in the Samaritan

Pentateuch rose above the fray of Catholic-Protestant polemics and focused on his well-known preoccupation with chronology. In 1624 Ussher received the first of six Samaritan Pentateuchs that were to come into his possession, and he graciously shared them with other savants in the British Isles.

Ussher did not respond to Morinus's comments on the Samaritan Pentateuch, probably because his own interests in the texts were so different, but by 1631, other non-Catholic scholars unleashed a massive counterattack against Morinus. Simon de Muis published three anti-Morinus works within a few years. The first, *Assertio veritatis hebraicae prima,* affirmed the superiority of the Hebrew text over the Samaritan or Greek. The other volumes developed the theme. Joining these works were several publications of Johannes Buxtorf, professor of Old Testament at Basel, who argued that the Hebrew vowel points and characters were at least as old as Ezra. In 1644, Johannes Henricus Hottengerus continued the attack on Morinus in his *Exercitationes anti-Morinianae de Pentateucho Samaritano,* and a decade later Arnold Boates, an English scholar of many interests, kept the controversy alive with his *Vindiciae veritatis hebraicae.*

That most of these attacks on Morinus rested on religious rather than scholarly presuppositions is apparent from the fact that the opposition was exclusively Protestant and passionate in its defense of the infallibility of inspired Scripture. Correspondence during this period is even more vehement than publications. Francis Taylor wrote to Ussher in the late 1630s referring to Morinus as the "false Catholic and Dosithean." Twenty years later Ussher received a letter from Boates chiding Morinus and his "adulterine Samaritan Pentateuch."

Both sides looked for places where the Samaritan text supported their argument and ignored the rest. In other words, no one carried out a thorough, systematic examination of the text. Morinus assumed that the extensive agreement between the Septuagint and the Samaritan Pentateuch constituted a vote for the authenticity of these versions.

Wilhelm Gesenius pronounced a benediction on this quarrel with his classic study published in 1815.[1] He thought that both the Samaritan Pentateuch and the Septuagint derived from a common Alexandrino-Samaritanus recension that differed from the Masoretic Text, a view that still has a few supporters today. But he developed ten categories of variants in the Samaritan text that have established its derivative nature.

A century later Paul Kahle argued that the Samaritan Pentateuch has older roots than Gesenius allowed.[2] That recognition opened the way for a

---

[1] Wihelm Gesenius, *De pentateuchi samaritani origine, indole, et auctoritate commentatio philologico-critica* (Halle: Rengerian, 1815).

[2] Paul Kahle, "Untersuchungen zur Geschichte des Pentateuchtextes," *TSK* 88 (1915): 399–439.

more sophisticated and complicated understanding of the variant recensions that developed, a development that the discoveries of the Dead Sea Scrolls at Qumran have helpfully illuminated.

The Samaritan Pentateuch shows evidence of attempts to clarify many of the difficult readings of the Hebrew text preserved by Jews in Jerusalem. These are the readings that generated the categories for Gesenius. The major points of intentional difference between the two texts relate to the Samaritan concern to establish the priority of Mount Gerizim. The most dramatic examples are the addition of the commandment to build an altar at Mount Gerizim (which Samaritans presumably added to Exod 20:17) and the reading of "Gerizim" for "Ebal" as the place where Moses commands an altar to be built in Deuteronomy 27:4. Many prefer the Samaritan reading of the latter verse.

While most of the Samaritan pentateuchal manuscripts are written in Hebrew, it is not uncommon for Aramaic or Arabic or both to appear in adjoining columns. Texts also exist with only the Arabic or the Aramaic. Nicholas Peiresc, who had been instrumental in bringing many Near Eastern manuscripts to Europe in the seventeenth century, took a keen interest in the Arabic Samaritan Pentateuch and sought both to obtain more copies and to convince more scholars of their value. Haseeb Shehadeh publishes works on the Arabic translation of the Samaritan Pentateuch; Jean-Pierre Rothschild has written about the Arabic manuscripts in the Bibliothèque Nationale; and Abraham Tal has written significant studies of the Aramaic Targum in several works, including a critical edition.[3]

With few exceptions, notably the Abisha scroll and scrolls made in the early twentieth century for tourists, the pentateuchal manuscripts are in codex (book) form. All of the older surviving copies are on animal skin, often from beasts offered as peace offerings. Most modern copies use paper.

CHARACTERISTICS OF MANUSCRIPTS

The total number of surviving pentateuchal manuscripts numbers in the hundreds, although fewer than one hundred date earlier than the eighteenth century and many of them consist only of fragments. The earliest date from about the ninth century C.E. (the probable dating for the Abisha scroll), and new ones continue to appear, even if production peaked in the fourteenth and fifteenth centuries. The largest collections reside at the synagogue

---

[3] Abraham Tal, *The Samaritan Targum of the Torah: A Critical Edition* (3 vols.; Tel Aviv: Tel Aviv University, 1980–1983).

at Nablus, the John Rylands Library at the University of Manchester, the British Museum, the Bibliothèque Nationale, Michigan State University, and a few private collections like that of David Sassoon.

The financial value of manuscripts before modern times is difficult to determine. In addition to identifying the buyer and seller and the date and the locale of the purchase, bills of sale for each of the five books within a pentateuchal manuscript often tell the price at which it was sold. Manuscripts varied in price from low teens to close to a hundred dirhems. At the beginning of the twentieth century a contemporary pentateuchal manuscript cost as little as twenty-five dollars, but museum records also indicate that E. K. Warren paid fifteen hundred dollars for CW 2478a and five hundred dollars for CW 2484. Warren himself describes a payment of one thousand dollars for a Pentateuch manuscript, probably CW 2473. In more recent times Samaritan manuscripts have entered the collector's world defined by Sotheby's, and prices have increased considerably. Alan Crown has drawn three conclusions about prices of manuscripts during the Renaissance:

> (1) Prices tended to fall rather than rise in the lifetime of the manuscript. (2) Prices rose or fell in response to market values, which included the number of manuscripts coming onto the market, fashions in manuscript writing, whether the manuscript was in more than one script or language, and its condition. (3) By and large the status of the scribe had no effect on the market price.[4]

Some attempts have succeeded at clustering Pentateuch manuscripts into families that have sufficiently common characteristics to indicate geographical, chronological, or scribal relationship. Two attempts at grouping manuscripts have been particularly fruitful. Simply on the basis of a predilection for horizontal dots, vertical dots, or dashes as punctuation, three groups of manuscripts separate out. Of the sample used, von Gall's D, F, and Gothic E group cluster, and they are the oldest of the set. A second group, von Gall's A, B, C, N, Q, and Gothic B go together and, with the exception of the anomalous C, represent fourteenth-century manuscripts from Damascus. The Egyptian manuscripts G, H, I, P, and Gothic A and I gather in another group.[5]

The most distinctive profiles were the result of a computer sorting by selected items in the text (plene readings, exchange of gutturals, omission of the definite article, and substitution of ' for ת as a suffix). One group included A, B, D, F, and G, which, with the exception of D, date to the mid-

---

[4] Alan Crown, "Studies in Samaritan Scribal Practices and Manuscript History: I. Manuscript Prices and Values," *BJRL* 65 (1983): 72–94.

[5] R. T. Anderson, "Clustering Samaritan Hebrew Pentateuchal Manuscripts," in *Étude samaritaines Pentateuque et Targum, éxègese et philologie, chroniques* (ed. Jean-Pierre Rothschild and Guy Dominique Sixdenier; Louvain-Paris: Peeters, 1988), 57–66.

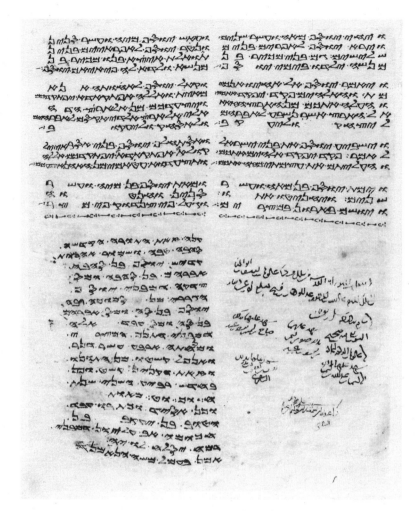

Last page of Genesis in CW 2478a. This is the manuscript for which E. K. Warren paid $1,500 early in the twentieth century. In the space below the biblical text is a bill of sale in both Samaritan Hebrew and Arabic. *Courtesy of Special Collections, Michigan State University Libraries.*

fourteenth century. The much earlier D may be the model from which the later manuscripts of that group derive. These two sets of data may indicate that punctuation was a function of geography while the time period had more effect on readings.

Sizes of pentateuchal manuscripts vary considerably (CW2482, for example, displays 35–37 lines on a rectangle 6.5 cm x 3.5 cm), but a page of about 35 cm x 38 cm is pretty standard. Prior to the eighteenth century, a scribe would mark out the lines with a bone or metal stylus that penetrated one side of the skin (usually the flesh side) sufficiently to leave its mark on the other side as well. Beginning about the eighteenth century a device called a *mastara* allowed one to impress several lines at once. In either case, the scribe then hung the letters from the top of the lines "like clothes pegged to a clothesline" as Robertson puts it.[6]

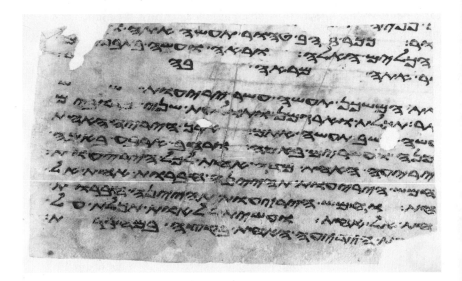

Manuscript fragment CW 2478b showing incised lines from which the letters are hung and, in lines 4 and 12, a single letter set apart to justify the left margin. Later manuscripts used two letters rather than one. *Courtesy of Special Collections, Michigan State University Libraries.*

The size of the margins, lines per page, and letters per line vary considerably among manuscripts. The text itself is written in majuscule (large) Samaritan characters in Arabic, or frequently in Arabic using Samaritan characters. The scribe preserves the justification of the left-hand margin by placing the last letter or two of each line at the left margin and spacing the remainder of the line so that any gaps occur in the middle of the line.

The text is divided into paragraphs, *qsym,* punctuated at the end by a double dot and a dash -: or by some more elaborate variation. Usually a blank space separates *qsym,* although it is not unusual for the last word of a *qsh* to run over that space. The major punctuation within a *qsh* is the double vertical dot : signifying the end of a sentence. Double horizontal dots .. serve as subdividers within the sentence, for direct address, and for other breaks. Other signs are used for questions: c, <, c, <, c:, <: ; vowel values -, *, .,’ ; and accent marks.

[6] Robertson, *Catalogue,* 2:xix.

Various signs separate larger units of reading, the most common being a simple bar with small vertical lines at each end like a horizontal capital "I."

The scribes usually belong to identifiable scribal families and range in age from teenagers to octogenarians who have copied from one to more than fifty pentateuchal manuscripts. One industrious family produced ninety-three pentateuchal manuscripts in about half a century. A production rate of about four hundred lines a day was common.

Scribes often intentionally created vertical columns of similar letters or whole words by leaving spaces in a line to assure the proper alignment. From three to nine *lamedhs,* for example, can appear in a vertical row that is visually arresting. Much of the page-to-page columnization is decoration subject to the whim of the scribe. A tradition of marking certain passages with columns of words developed probably because the selected words constituted a passage providing visual "bookmarks" through the otherwise unbroken text.

Most Pentateuchs contain at least one acrostic and bill of sale that reveal data on people, habitations, manuscript production, contemporary events like natural disasters, and social organization. The acrostics are woven into the biblical text, usually in Deuteronomy. The scribe accomplishes this by marking out a central channel down the page, one letter wide, into which he then drops letters from the biblical text to create a message running vertically through the biblical text. The scribe must often skip several lines before the desired letter comes up sufficiently close to the channel to be moved into it. The entire exercise requires great skill. Characteristically the scribe tells his name, the date of completion, the commissioner of the manuscript, and the location of production. Occasionally we catch some glimpse into the historical context of production. For example, the revered Abisha scroll contains an acrostic extending and drawing from letters in the biblical text from Deuteronomy 6:10 to 13:9. Although some of the letters are problematic,[7] it apparently reads:

אני אבישע בן פינחס בן אלעזר בן אהרן הכהן להם רצון יהוה וכבודי
כתבתי ספר הקדש בפתח אהל מועד בהרגריזים שנת שלשה עשר
בני ישראל ארץ כנען לכל גבולותיה סביב אודה את יהוה אמן
למלכות

I am Abisha son of Pinhas son of Eleazar son of Aaron the priest; on them be the favor of the Lord and his glory.
I wrote this holy book at the door of the tent of meeting on Mount Gerizim in the year thirteen of the reign of the children of Israel in the land of Canaan to all its boundaries round about. I praise the Lord. Amen.

---

[7] Crown, "Abisha Scroll," 49.

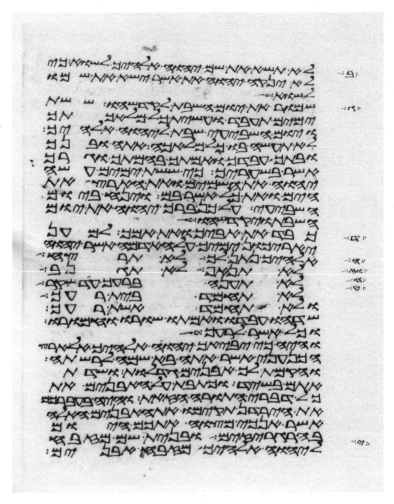

A page from CW 2484 showing intentional spreading of text to allow letters to align
vertically, particularly in four lines just below the center of the page. The characters in the
right margin number the second through tenth commandments, which appear on the page.
Courtesy of Special Collections, Michigan State University Libraries.

A bill of sale, meanwhile, is simply written in paragraph form immediately following a biblical book. Such documents include the name of the seller and purchaser, the date of the transaction, and occasionally the price. Witnesses usually also attest the sale. The bills are replete with honorific titles that give clues to the age, status, and sometimes the vocation of the persons described.

The following bill of sale appears at the end of the book of Exodus in Chamberlain-Warren 2478a:

A page in Leviticus from CW 2473 showing an acrostic running vertically through the center of the page. *Courtesy of Special Collections, Michigan State University Libraries.*

קני זאת התורה הקדושה סמוך קהלה וארכון

קהלה יוסף בן סהבה וסמוך קהלה ועשה טובה

עבד יהוה בן עבד היהוב דמבני איקרה מן סהבה

וסמוך קהלה וארכון קהלה ויעדוה ועשה טובה

עבד יהוה בן וסמוך וקהלה ועשה טובה

עבד היהוב בן צדקה דמבני רמח וכהלון מן

שכוני מצרים בארבעה ועשרים דנר בחדש רגב שנת

שנים ותשעים ושמנה מאות תהיה בריכה עליו אמן

וכתב אברהם בן אבי עזי בן יוסף בן יתרנה מן דמשך

This Holy Torah was bought by (..)[8](..)(..)
(..) Joseph son of (..)(..)(..)(..)(..)(..)
Obadiah son of Abd Hehob of the family Iqara from (..)
(..)(..)(..)(..)(..)(..)(..)
Obadiah son of (..)(..)(..)(..)(..)(..)
Abd Hehob son of Sedaqa of the family Remach, all of them from
among the inhabitants of Egypt, for 24 dinars in the month of Rajab in the
year 892 (C.E. 1487). May there be a blessing upon it. Amen.
Abraham son of Ab Uzzi son of Joseph son of Jitrana of Damascus wrote this.

The honorific titles in both acrostics and bills of sale abound, often doubling the length of a note, burying personal names in a sea of predictable if not fully understandable adjectives. Few catalogues make much of them. Von Gall and Sassoon reproduce them in Samaritan Hebrew, but do not translate them. Robertson indicates their presence with a series of dots and parentheses, but offers no translation. Ben Zvi writes in Hebrew and so offers no translation. Robertson helpfully discusses the meaning of twenty (there are more than one hundred) of these titles,[9] and assistance with some others comes from the glossary in A. Cowley's work on Samaritan liturgies.[10] Most of the titles nevertheless remain untranslated and in various degrees of obscurity.

The majority of the manuscripts come from four primary centers: Damascus, Egypt, Shechem, and Zarephath. Twice as many come from Damascus as from any other place, reflecting the size and relative security of that community for much of its history. Egypt was the home of the prolific Munes family that produced the largest number of known manuscripts, mainly in the forty-one-year period between 1468 and 1509. That Shechem produced a fair share of the manuscripts is not surprising since it was the chief holy place of the sect. That more were not produced attests to the insecurity of that city and the necessity for frequent and extensive emigration to other places, notably Egypt and Damascus.

Scribes associated with Zarephath produced several manuscripts, all copied between 1160 and 1225. The attraction of this coastal town, which was presumably involved in the intrigues among Syrians, Egyptians, and Crusaders, raises issues about the Samaritans that the little available data cannot answer.

If we accept the accuracy of the scribal dating, the earliest dated manuscript, after the Abisha scroll, is Ben Zvi's *daleth* from 1065. Production

---

[8] Bracketed double dots indicate an honorific title.
[9] Edward Robertson, "Notes and Extracts from the Semitic Manuscripts in the John Rylands Library," *BJRL* 21 (1937): 240–72.
[10] Cowley, *Samaritan Liturgy*.

peaked in the fourteenth and fifteenth centuries. From the ninety-year period between 1231 and 1321, not a single manuscript survives. That fact may be silent testimony to the turmoil characterizing the struggle among Crusaders, Mongols, Mamluks, and Arabs. By contrast, the most prosperous period occurred at the end of the fifteenth century. The eleven-year period between 1474 and 1485 produced an unusual quantity of manuscripts.

Several Samaritan biblical commentaries survive, including Rylands Items 131–34 by Muslim, 135 by Ghazal, 136–39 by Muslim, 140 by Ghazal, and 142–43 by Abu Hasan.

COMPARISON OF THE SAMARITAN PENTATEUCH AND THE MASORETIC TEXT

Advances in textual criticism, amelioration of Roman Catholic-Protestant tensions, and the discovery of the fragments of diverse biblical texts at Qumran have provided the data and created the climate for new perspectives on the Samaritan Pentateuch and its role in biblical studies. The Samaritan Pentateuch evolved relatively independently from the Masoretic Text around the Hasmonean period (653–142 B.C.E.), even if all text types remained flexible for at least a couple of centuries. Some Qumran manuscript pieces relate to Samaritan text types. Only by the second century C.E. do we have a more or less fixed Samaritan text.

Jean Morin's arguments that the Samaritan Pentateuch predates the Masoretic Text are no longer accepted. For example, he argued, rightly, that the Samaritan alphabetic characters are more ancient than the Hebrew block letters, but draws the wrong conclusion from this fact: in truth, the Samaritans merely preserved ancient forms of letters. Likewise, it is true that the Samaritan Pentateuch agrees with the Septuagint in almost two thousand readings against the Masoretic Text. Nevertheless, the Samaritan Pentateuch is even more closely related to the Masoretic Text than to the Septuagint.[11]

The similarities to the Septuagint should not be ignored, however. Both the Samaritan Pentateuch and the Septuagint may have grown out of an earlier common source, as Gesenius argued. The relationship between them may be the reason even for scribal practices in the two textual traditions. For example, Codex Alexandrinus (a fourth century C.E. copy of the Septuagint) uses a pattern of interlaced zigzag lines running horizontally across the page to mark the end of a biblical book. The same decorative pattern appears in

---

[11] Bruce Waltke, "Prolegomena to the Samaritan Pentateuch" (Ph.D. diss., Harvard University, 1965), 226–56.

many Samaritan Pentateuchs. Samaritan Pentateuchs also follow the model of Alexandrinus in the marking of parallel texts, the Decalogue structure, and use of *kai/waw* symmetry,[12] further indication that the two are somehow related.

What, then, is the value of the Samaritan Pentateuch? For biblical scholarship it has been a major catalyst in textual criticism. Its arrival in a Europe ripe with knowledge of Semitic languages triggered the major ascent of textual criticism. Scholars' motives may have been sectarian, but the fervent struggle to establish the text finally cut across denominational lines and put textual criticism on a sound footing.[13]

Canonical critics find here an extensive case study of how sectarian groups adapt received texts to legitimate the rituals and ideologies of their beliefs. The Samaritan text is replete with alterations responding to the needs of the community. The extended comments on Mount Gerizim constitute the most obvious example.

The Samaritan Pentateuch also supports the Documentary Hypothesis for the origins of the Pentateuch. Tracing the evolution of the text using a Proto-Samaritan text type, the Masoretic Text, and the full-fledged Samaritan text, Jeffrey Tigay has demonstrated a method of composition by the combination of texts that the Documentary Hypothesis postulated.[14]

The Samaritan Pentateuch, finally, should interest sociologists and anthropologists as an artifact that has molded its community of readers for at least two thousand years. The survival of any community as a distinct subculture for that long is dramatic. The group's very existence is ample testimony to the power and influence of the Samaritan Pentateuch. For the Samaritans the text is the central religious artifact that has sanctioned the beliefs and practices of their religion.

---

[12] It is common in Samaritan pentateuchal manuscripts for the scribe to manipulate the words and letters in a series of lines so certain letters will be lined up vertically. The Hebrew letter *waw* is a common letter to use in such a line. Codex Alexandrinus exhibits the same characteristic with the Greek equivalent word, *kai*. See Alan Crown, "Studies in Samaritan Scribal Practices and Manuscript History III: Columnar Writing and the Samaritan Massorah," *BJRL* 67 (1984): 349–81.

[13] Moshe Goshen-Gottstein, "The Textual Criticism of the Old Testament: Rise, Decline, Rebirth," *JBL* 102 (1983): 372–75.

[14] Jeffrey H. Tigay, "An Empirical Basis for the Documentary Hypothesis," *JBL* 94 (1975): 327–42

Chapter 9

Samaritan Religion

CREED

The Samaritan creed succinctly outlines the faith's basic beliefs: "We say: My faith is in thee, YHWH; and in Moses son of Amram, thy servant; and in the Holy Law; and in Mount Gerizim Bethel; and in the Day of Vengeance and Recompense."[1] Montgomery and MacDonald[2] have noted the close parallel between this creed and that of Islam. Samaritan theology was formulated in dialogue with Islam (as it had been earlier with Christianity and Judaism). Still, there is a certain internal logic to the creeds: God, the prophet who revealed God, and the hope for the future. Judaism is content to stop with the affirmation of God. The unique Christian creedal omission concerns Scripture. The unique Samaritan addition is affirmation of Mount Gerizim, a critical distinction between the sect and Judaism.

Monotheism

The Samaritan concept of God parallels the rigorous monotheism of Judaism and Islam, resisting a multiform presence like the Christian Trinity or the emanations of Gnosticism. They share the Muslim affirmation "There is no God, but God" and use it extensively in their services and writings. El or Ela is the normal name for God (akin to Islamic Allah). While the Tetragrammaton, YHWH, is also in normal use, Samaritans seldom employ Elohim, the name regularly used by Jews. Samaritans, like Jews, avoid making images and even avoid applying the anthropomorphic concept of father to God, whom they see as the ineffable and incorporeal creator and sustainer who has entered into unique covenant with Israel. Samaritans thus surpass Judaism in eschewing anthropomorphism. As we noted in the discussion of the Chamberlain-Warren inscription 2472, the Samaritan text of Exodus 15:3 replaces the more explicitly anthropomorphic "man" as a description of God with "warrior." The Samaritan targums exhibit the same tendency,

---

[1] Montgomery, *Samaritans,* 207.
[2] John MacDonald, *The Theology of the Samaritans* (London: SCM, 1964), 53.

nicely shown in Exodus 24:10ff., where one fears God or is present with him rather than seeing him. Montgomery notes that the Arabic translation of Abu'l Fath's chronicle has approximately six hundred instances of such anthropomorphisms.[3]

In the same vein, Samaritans insist that God does not tire or age. They join Muslims in responding negatively to the Jewish and Christian Scriptures that describe God resting on the seventh day in Genesis or being roused from sleep in Psalms. Samaritan thought thus dodges the theological problems that these texts present.

Like Muslims, Samaritans also use multiple epithets to refer to God. Muslims usually attribute ninety-nine names to Allah. The longest list of names for God in Samaritan literature occurs in an acrostic with four names from each letter of the alphabet, for a total of eighty-eight.[4] God is, for example, Creator, the Existent One, King, Redeemer, Victor, and the Wise.

God is infinite with a boundless past and future. God is most profoundly revealed in two great acts, the creation and the giving of the Torah. Many hymns of creation appear in various liturgies. In them God creates everything, even the *tohu-wa-bohu* or primordial chaos out of which creation arises. On the first day God created the light (Holy Spirit) which is from God rather than of God (contrast the view of the Gnostics). Marqe describes seven gates within the ultimate gate from which light moves in a series of manifestations. Despite the explicit denial, these meditations on light invite comparison with the meaning of light in Gnosticism and in the Johannine school.[5]

When Samaritan theology argues for the existence of God, it does so mainly within the confines of the cosmological argument, postulating God as the primary or first causal factor in the world. This approach mirrors the Christian Hermetic tradition of the late Middle Ages, which saw nature as a reflection of God. This view also anticipated contemporary process theology with its assumption that God continues to be at work in the movements of nature. A continuing line of cause and effect unfolds in the world.

Samaritan theology gravitates from philosophical foci to traditional images of power and justice—God as king and God as judge—images that transcend and impose themselves upon weak and sinful humanity. A profound humility in the Samaritan approach to God exists, with angels filling the vast space between deity and humanity. Epiphanius, a fourth-century bishop of

---

[3] Montgomery, *Samaritans*, 211.
[4] Montgomery, *Samaritans*, 215.
[5] Although MacDonald has a rich discussion of the use of light in Samaritan theology and parallels with Gnosticism, he also says, "We can find no true Gnosticism in the Samaritan religion at all" (*Theology*, 453).

Salamis, wrote that the sect did not believe in angels. Presumably his opinion reflected the views of persons that he knew, but angels do appear regularly in subsequent Samaritan literature. An eighteenth-century response to a direct question from the Frenchman de Sacy confessed: "We believe in the holy angels who are in the heavens."[6] The liturgy and *Memar Marqe* posit several qualities of the angels. The concept of angels helps to reduce the use of anthropomorphic language in talking about God, a serious concern in Samaritan theology, and provides a link across the gulf between finitude and infinity. Angels do not eat or drink. They are created beings with some relationship to the stars. There are several ranks, each with special duties to perform. Abul Hasan al-Suri in his *Kitab al-Tabbah* says that their bodies are almost bodiless spirits. They have no internal organs, do not work, and know nothing of evil. Abul Hasan talks about one type of angel, the cherubim, who do not resemble humans and have only appeared to Moses. Other types have no analogy on earth.

Moses

Moses, as the mediator of the Torah, is the third focus of Samaritan adoration. The group's beliefs about him reflect strongly, again, a dialogue with Christian and Islamic cultures. Samaritan theology blossomed in this rich milieu and fully utilized a rich vocabulary available for describing religious founders.

MacDonald, both in his introduction to the *Memar Marqe*[7] and his work on Samaritan theology,[8] points to several closely corresponding developments in Christianity and Samaritanism. Parallel stories and beliefs about Moses and Jesus are particularly telling. Marqe says, "He who believes in Moses believes in his Lord,"[9] a close parallel to John 14:1, "You believe in God, believe also in me." Moses' role as the true prophet of God in one religion closely resembles Jesus' in the other, or Muhammed's in Islam, for that matter. Blessings invoke "the name of Moses the faithful," the last and most exalted of the prophets. One might say that just as early Christians attempted to make Jesus a second Moses, the Samaritans sought to make Moses a second Jesus. MacDonald concludes that the basic framework of similarity is that both "Moses and Christ were with God in the beginning, were in communion and communication with him during their earthly life, and

---

[6] De Sacy, "Correspondance des Samaritains," 106 (text), 121 (translation).

[7] MacDonald, *Memar Marqah*, ch. 18.

[8] MacDonald, *Memar Marqah*, 150–57, and ch. 22 entitled "Moses and Christ" in the same volume extensively examine parallels between the two religions.

[9] MacDonald, *Memar Marqah*, 160.

were fully restored to their glorified state after death, there to abide for ever-
more, still lord over the House of God."[10]

Moses' death draws little attention, but his birth is exalted in a treatise
by Ismail Ramihi entitled *Molad Mosheh* ("Birth of Moses"). It is a rhymed
eulogy to Moses depicting him as a preexistent primordial light who came to
illuminate the world as the final gate of light entering the world. Many other
poems praise his various attributes. Liturgies exalt him in phrases usually reserved for God. For example, one liturgical passage reads, "Who is like our
master Moses?"[11] analogous to the much used text (included on the Chamberlain-Warren inscription) of Exodus 15:11, "Who is like you, O Lord,
among the gods?" The restorer who will come as the agent of God will be one
like Moses.

A wide diversity of literature about him developed in Islamic times. *Al-
Asatir* ("Stories") of Moses, an Aramaic work of about the eleventh or twelfth
century, preserves ancient traditional stories of the early patriarchs paralleled
in the Old Testament pseudepigrapha. The work is a haggadic supplement
to the Pentateuch, a story amplifying the biblical text. This text earned the
Samaritans' high regard because tradition claimed that Moses had written it.
Z. Ben-Hayyim has published a translation and modern commentary.

Torah

Many modern travelers to the Samaritan synagogue at Nablus leave
with a photograph of an ancient handwritten manuscript in an elegant brass
scroll case, flanked on either side by a Samaritan priest. A priest hands the
tourist a card claiming that this uniquely significant artifact is the Abisha
scroll, a copy of the Torah. The scroll gets its name from its alleged copyist,
Abisha the great-grandson of Aaron, the brother of Moses. Although the
scroll almost certainly dates to the end of the first millennium C.E., it is still
the most powerful Samaritan symbol for their awe-inspiring Torah. The Pentateuch stands in sanctity second only to God. It defines the location of the
holy place and the services performed there and elsewhere. It establishes the
qualifications for the priesthood, and the text's interpretation is the source of
priestly status. Every service centers upon the reverent reading of Torah. Its
words are carved in stone to decorate synagogues and carefully copied by
hand on parchment or fine paper to be passed down from one generation to
another.

---

[10] MacDonald, *Memar Marqah*, 446.
[11] Robertson, *Catalogue*, 1:125.

The Torah not only points to God; it is intimately a part of the God who wrote and delivered it to Moses. One prostrates oneself before the Torah as one would in the divine presence. The scroll sits housed in a niche called an altar, the place where the divine contacts this world.

Mount Gerizim

Marqe, that prominent Samaritan theologian of the early Christian era, asked rhetorically, "Why was Mount Gerizim called Har ha-Kedem (the ancient or eastern mountain)?" and answers, "Because it was a twin of the Garden of Eden. Both were revealed when the dry land was uncovered and Adam's form was made from the dust of the Mount." Abel built the first altar there, and Abraham brought Isaac there for sacrifice. Among Marqe's multiple lists is a category of the "Best Things in the World." Among them is Mount Gerizim, which deserves to have thirteen names.

In Samaritan tradition, Mount Gerizim is the oldest, the most central, and the highest mountain in the world, towering above the Great Flood and providing the land on which Noah could land his ark. An astonished visitor to Mount Gerizim is puzzled by that tradition:

"Obviously there are many higher mountains," the visitor exclaims.

"No," an unperturbed Samaritan responds. "Mount Gerizim is the tallest mountain in the world."

"Look across the valley," the visitor persists, "even Mount Ebal is taller than Gerizim. How can you deny that?"

"Because," the Samaritan patiently explains, "Mount Gerizim is the tallest mountain in the world."[12]

The significant scriptural base for the importance of Gerizim appears in Deuteronomy 27:4. The Masoretic Text reads: "So when you have crossed over the Jordan, you shall set up these stones, about which I am commanding you today, on Mount Ebal, and you shall cover them with plaster." The Samaritan version, however, reads "Gerizim" in place of "Ebal." Discussion as to which group altered the text tends to suspect the Samaritans, who have the most to gain from doing so.[13]

---

[12] Adapted from Millar Burrows, *What Mean These Stones?* (New York: Meridian, 1957), 278.

[13] For a brief discussion of the reasons, see footnote 133 in Montgomery, *Samaritans,* 235.

At times Gerizim has been a lightening rod inviting disaster upon the Samaritans. John Hyrcanus destroyed the sanctuary on the mount in 128 B.C.E. Between 26 and 36 C.E., an unnamed figure rallied a large group of Samaritans to climb the mountain, promising to show them the sacred vessels that the high priest Uzzi had hidden there (according to Abu'l Fath; Josephus says it was Moses who hid them). Pontius Pilate blocked their way with a strong military force and killed or captured many of them. Later in the century Samaritans fleeing oppression gathered by the thousands at their sacred place and held the Romans at bay for a month before their water ran out. Those who did not die of thirst were slaughtered by the enemy. Both Josephus and a Samaritan inscription[14] preserve that story. In each case Vespasian dispatched a general (Cerealis according to Josephus, Trajan in the Samaritan inscription) who laid siege to the mountain until the water ran out and then slaughtered 11,600 people (ten thousand according to the Samaritans).

The Samaritan *Book of Joshua* and Abu'l Fath both tell the charming story of a bronze bird crafted by the Romans to assure that no Samaritan could ascend the Mount, lest he trigger the bird to call out, "Hebrews!" The Samaritan sage, Baba Raba, as already described, devised a plan to deceive the bird and have it destroyed.

In the fifth century Zeno drove the Samaritans from Gerizim and either modified an existing structure or built a church dedicated to Mary on the highest peak. The Samaritans later destroyed the church, but Justinian built another about 530.

A German traveler in the mid-nineteenth century heard from the high priest that the source of all the rivers of the world lies within Gerizim and that at one time the fountainhead of the Tigris inside that mountain had to be unclogged because the waters were not reaching Baghdad and Basra.[15] However implausible the geological lesson, the religious significance of Mount Gerizim becomes unambiguous. The messiah will reign from there, and it will be the setting for the Last Judgment. Joseph, the ancestor of the Samaritans, inherited the mountain according to their chronicles, and the traditional site of his burial is at its foot. Joshua built an altar, a temple, and a fortress there.

Historians of religion could not ask for a clearer example of a sacred mountain as navel of the earth, where heaven and earth meet. In Judges 9:37, Gaal exclaims, "Look, men are coming down from *tabbur haares* (the navel of the earth)." Certainly the Samaritan community has derived sustenance throughout its history from its proximity to the mountain. At the turn of this century only the community at Gerizim survived. Whenever possible (or necessary), the Samaritans returned there. Their documents attest nearly a dozen synagogues within a ten-mile radius of Gerizim.

---

[14] Strugnell, "Quelques inscriptions samaritaines," 562–71.
[15] Schur, *History of the Samaritans,* 173.

There were times when the ruling powers prohibited the Samaritans any access to the mountain. According to Abu'l Fath, Simon, the brother of John Hyrcanus, had forbidden its use even before it was devastated. The Roman emperor Hadrian (117–138 C.E.) built a large and lavish temple to Zeus on the sacred place. In the seventeenth century, the sultan Mehmed IV (1648–1687) forbade access to the mount, and the annual Passover sacrifice had to be offered on its eastern slope. During the decade 1840–1850, the Samaritans abandoned the site because of a lack of security.

The mutually exclusive claims of Gerizim and Jerusalem, also a navel of the earth according to its devotees, define a distinctive difference between Jews and Samaritans, though some would caution against overstating its significance.[16]

When accessible, Gerizim has been the site of the three pilgrimage festivals of the Samaritans: Passover-Massot, Shavuot, and Sukkot. To accommodate travelers staying between Passover and Massot, permanent houses have replaced the tents of former times, a signal that, for the time being, Mount Gerizim remains the anchor of the community.

Day of Vengeance and Recompense

In the Samaritan scheme of history, the coming time of divine favor will replace the current period of divine disfavor. The idea is akin to the Jewish (including Qumran) and Christian distinction between an apocalyptic present evil age and a redemptive age about to come. For the Samaritans, the original period of divine favor was present in the early days of the settlement of Palestine when the tabernacle rested in its proper place on Mount Gerizim. That period ended when the Jews withdrew and Eli moved the sanctuary to Shiloh. Early Samaritan groups disputed whether the original period of divine favor began with Moses (so the *Asatir*) or with Joshua (as in the *Book of Joshua*). The subsequent secession of the northern kingdom by Jeroboam and the establishment of a sanctuary at Bethel further justified God's anger. God turned away (hence *Fanutah*, "to turn away") and left Gerizim, initiating the period of divine disfavor. God instructed Uzzi to put the holy vessels and garments into a cave and seal it. The cave subsequently disappeared to await the *Ra'utah*, or return of God's favor, when God will return to the tent on Mount Gerizim.

The eschatology of the Samaritans resembles that of other heirs of the Israelite tradition. The messiah will inaugurate a coming Day of the Lord characterized by a long period of peace and security before the final end. The

---

[16] For example, Coggins, *Samaritans and Jews*, 113.

idea of the Day of the Lord has a long and complex history. First mentioned in Amos and then frequently in the prophets, the concept has roots in holy war, perhaps a specific day of intervention by God, but also in eschatological expectations of cosmic judgment. Both connotations are implicit in Samaritan thought.

This eschatological scheme developed over many centuries, integrating concepts that probably had separate origins. Unfortunately we catch glimpses of the process only occasionally, particularly during the revitalization of the third and fourth centuries, the late Middle Ages, and the modern period. The three key components are, again, the era of divine favor *(Ra'utah)*, the Taheb, and the kingdom.

According to the *Durran,* the harbinger of the period of divine favor will be initiated by the Taheb, a cryptic term for a figure whose role follows Deuteronomy 18:18. He is a human being (unlike the Christian messiah). Samaritans avoid the problem of the relationship of the Taheb to the divine, but disagree regarding his ancestry: Noah, Jacob, Seth, Pinhas, and Moses are contenders. A literal rendering of Deuteronomy 18:18 implies a Moses redivivus, but the Taheb is also associated with Joshua in the Samaritan *Book of Joshua* and with Joseph according to Marqe. The posing of Joshua and Joseph as alternatives probably reflects Samaritan sectarianism, although the two ancestors share in common the fact that each lived 110 years, the period of time that the Taheb is to rule. This figure's role changed from prophetic to priestly during the Middle Ages, creating an ambiguity that continues to the present. Only when the community repents will he present his credentials, three significant artifacts from the past: the staff of Aaron, unspoiled manna, and the tabernacle. The period from Adam to the Taheb will be six thousand years.

The Samaritan hope for the future focuses on the Day of Reward, when the faithful will enter the garden of Eden, characterized as a city both at its beginning and at its end. Eden thus plays for Samaritans the role that Jews and Christians assign to the heavenly Jerusalem. Those who argue that the New Testament book of Hebrews addressed a Samaritan audience note that Hebrews 11:10 intentionally leaves ambiguous the identity of the "city which has foundations." Jews could assume it was Jerusalem, and Samaritans that it was the "city in which God's goodness dwelled from the beginning."

Originally the idea of a Taheb, or prophet like Moses, and that of a second kingdom, were independent from the notion of the *Ra'utah,* but probably during the Middle Ages the three concepts merged into a single vision of hope for the future. The second kingdom becomes either the period of the Taheb (see Marqe) or an unlimited eternal, earthly, ideal kingdom.

At first the Samaritans, much like the Sadducees, resisted the notion of resurrection, but in time they came to believe that their dead would join the community on Mount Gerizim on the day of vengeance and recompense.

PRIESTHOOD

There are several stories of the origin of the Samaritan priesthood. Both Jewish and Samaritan accounts of the sect's origins assign a significant role to the priests, but they are radically different stories. Second Kings 17 says that the people who later became the Samaritans, at least according to later Jewish reading of this source, were aliens whom the Assyrian Sargon II settled in the depopulated northern Palestine. These aliens survived attacks of lions only because priests of the original population taught them the ways of the local deity (2 Kgs 17:29–33).

For later Jews, such as Josephus, this story became crucial to identifying the Samaritans, even though this interpretation is clearly anachronistic. The Samaritans, in any case, tell another story. They claim that Judaism was the breakaway sect, an action that ended the *Radwan* (period of God's favor). This took place during the tenure of the sixth high priest, Ozzi. As already noted, Eli b. Yafni sought to usurp the high priesthood and convinced many followers to join him at Shiloh, where they built a temple, according to Abu'l Fath.[17]

Josephus tells still another story of the origin of priests of Mount Gerizim, calling them renegades from Jerusalem who fled because of their questionable moral character. Yet another interpretation is implied by the fact that the Samaritans refer to Gerizim as "Bethel," a name that, incidentally, would be anathema to southerners. Perhaps Bethel itself was the source of priests, as well as a name for Gerizim.

The subsequent record of the high priestly succession, known as the Chain, is part of Samaritan tradition. The present high priest is 147th from Adam or 121st from Aaron.[18] From the time of Baba Raba, priests outside the high-priestly lineage ceased to record their genealogies.

Tensions emerged at various times over the centuries, sometimes because of foreign rulers who exiled the priesthood, but more often because of intercommunity problems. Hesitancy among Samaritans to accept more of Scripture than the Torah may reflect the priestly attachment to a canon that sanctioned their status. The struggle between the priesthood and laity

---

[17] Stenhouse, *The Kitab al Tarikh of Abu'l Fath*, 47–48.
[18] Gaster, *Studies and Texts*, 1:493–502.

recurred. First-century sages challenged the priests, Baba Raba extended the power of the laity, but the most serious threat to the priesthood came in 1623–1624 when the direct line of Aaron ended with the death of the last male heir. The community adapted by replacing the Aaronites with priests of the tribe of Levi of the family of Uzziel, son of Kohath.

RITUAL

The Samaritan calendar of holidays is a puzzle that only the priest can unravel. Originally the feasts coincided with those of the Jewish calendar. However, calculation of the calendar became so complicated under influence from Byzantine and Arab practice that only the priest can determine the appropriate feast days for any given year. Robertson suggests that the difficulty of the system was a way of hiding information from the Christians.[19] Samaritans say the reckoning of the calendar is a secret God revealed to Adam. On the day of Simmuth, sixty days before Passover, each member of the community pays a half shekel and receives the calendar for the next six months.

During the year the Samaritans celebrate Passover, the Feast of Unleavened Bread, the Feast of Weeks, the Feast of the Seventh Month, Yom Kippur, the Feast of Booths, and "the eighty days of solemn assembly." The major synagogue festival is the Day of Atonement, when officiants read Torah and the Abisha scroll is exhibited for adoration. The community celebrates Passover, the related but distinct Festival of Unleavened Bread, the Feast of Weeks, and the Feast of Booths on Mount Gerizim. Although Passover is separate from Unleavened Bread, the Samaritans remain there through both.

Passover attracts most attention today, not only because it preserves the tradition of Deuteronomy but also because the community still practices the ancient ritual of animal sacrifice. Some form of this has been practiced for centuries, but extensive accounts of the service date only from the last two centuries. Preparation, including a two-week watching of the sacrificial lambs, begins several days before Passover. On the day itself, the community climbs the narrow path southwest of Nablus. They stop at several designated places to listen to readings of Scripture. In the past, they erected tents on top of Gerizim, but, as mentioned, permanent buildings have recently replaced them. The women remain in the shelters while the priests lead the men in the opening hymns as they all face the east. If Passover falls on a Sabbath, the service begins at sunset. Otherwise it begins in the early afternoon. The men usually wear white robes and sing ever more intensely as the priest reads the

---

[19] Robertson, *Catalogue,* 1:xxxv.

Passover story. When the sun sets, the priest should be at Exodus 12:6, and that verse ends a segment of the service. Oven fires are lit and seven to twenty lambs are brought up, the number depending on the size of the assembly. They are quickly slaughtered, and blood is sprinkled on the foreheads of the children. The community prays while it waits for the water to come to the boiling point. Then the sheep are fleeced, and most of the entrails are removed along with one shoulder and burned. After inspection for blemishes and then salting, the carcasses are ready to be roasted on spits.

Circumcision of males and celebration of the Sabbath are the common rituals of the Samaritans. Circumcision occurs on the eighth day after birth, following the morning prayers, and it includes the reading of a poem by Marqe recalling that circumcision is so important that the community performed it even during periods of extreme oppression. Sabbath is also strictly observed with regular services in the synagogue. Since the prayers are said in union (and with fervor), the services seemed to outsiders to be noisy.[20]

A funeral, which begins within twenty-four hours of death, starts at the home of the deceased. The women lament and the men carry the body in a simple coffin to the cemetery on Mount Gerizim, where they bury it to the accompaniment of prescribed prayers.[21]

All services, regular or not, use extensive readings from the Torah, hymns, and prayers. The earliest part of the liturgy is the *Defter*, a collection of Marqe's compositions, and hymns by his father, Amram Dare, and his son Nanah. The following prayer, said silently at the beginning of each Sabbath public service and festival, is an example from the *Defter*:

> In the Name of Yahweh the Great we begin and we end. Before Thee I stand at the gate of Thy mercies, Yahweh my God and God of my fathers to speak Thy praise and Thy glory according to my poor strength and my weakness. I know today and I have placed (it) at my heart that Thou Yahweh art the God in the heavens above, and on the earth beneath there is no other. Here before Thee I stand and I face the chosen place Mount Gerizim, Bethel-Luzah, the mountain of the inheritance and place which Thou hast made for Thee to dwell, O Yahweh, the sanctuary of Yahweh which Thine hands have established.[22]

The worshiper generally performs ablutions in preparation for prayer and stands with covered head and hands extended with palms upward. An officiant, usually a priest, leads the congregation in the chanting of the prayers.

With subsequent additions, the *Defter* constitutes the prayer book of the Samaritan community. More than one hundred liturgical manuscripts

---

[20] Schur, *History of the Samaritans*, 160–61.
[21] Reinhard Pummer, *The Samaritans* (Leiden: Brill, 1987), 19–20.
[22] John Bowman, *Samaritan Documents* (Pittsburgh: Pickwick Press, 1977), 332.

appear in catalogues of various Samaritan collections. They cover a range of festivals, already mentioned, as well as special occasions such as circumcision, marriage,[23] and burials. Much of every service is devoted to hymns, the longest of which are usually acrostics.[24]

SACRED PLACE

There is no doubt as to the sanctity of Mount Gerizim, but much controversy exists as to where the essential sanctity lies, whether in the altar, the tabernacle, the temple, or the mountain itself. The designation in the Samaritan creed of Gerizim as Bethel epitomizes the ambiguity. Is it a place name, a sanctuary, or a deity? W. F. Albright noted that Bethel was a Canaanite deity name that appeared 250 years later at Elephantine. Samaritans use it to refer to Gerizim on the grounds that it was here, they claim, that Jacob saw the ladder. Others have understood it to refer to the highest peak or the mountain itself.

All these ideas can claim some biblical support. Deuteronomy 27 includes a command to build an altar, and the *Tulidah* says that the high priest Abdiel led three hundred thousand Israelites out of exile and built an altar. Neither narrative mentions any other structure. But significance is also vested in the tabernacle that the Samaritans, with the support of Joshua 18:1 and 19:51, claim to have been atop Gerizim. According to Samaritan tradition, the tabernacle disappeared in the time of Eli, signaling the period of God's disfavor *(Fanuta)*. Subsequent stories tell of people going there to find the hidden materials with the hope of initiating the coming of the Taheb.

That mountain, altar, and tabernacle were significant no one questions. However, the existence of a temple is more problematic. Josephus[25] and the late Samaritan chronicles allude to a temple, but lack of archaeological evidence for such a structure complicates the problem. The perennial focus of excavations on Gerizim is the recovery of the Samaritan temple. F. de Saulcy and later V. Guerin stimulated the excavation of Gerizim during the late 1800s by identifying different sets of ruins as the remnants of the temple. In the mid-1870s, C. W. Wilson reported on ruins that he identified as a fortress and church built upon the site previously occupied by the temple. Wilson also mentioned a building on Tell er-Ras but left it unexamined. That structure remained untouched until the 1960s, when R. Bull excavated it (calling

---

[23] An extensive study of marriage contracts is found in Reinhard Pummer, *Samaritan Marriage Contracts and Deeds of Divorce* (2 vols.; Wiesbaden: Harrassowitz, 1993–1997).
[24] The standard treatment on Samaritan ritual is by Cowley, *Samaritan Liturgy.*
[25] *Ant.* 12.257–264; 13.74–79.

it Building A) and discovered underneath it a large platform of unhewn stone resting upon bedrock. This large platform (Building B), Bull identified as part of the temple and "the remains of the Samaritan altar of sacrifice."[26] The identification of Building B as the Samaritan temple or altar has been challenged by subsequent excavations, and even the existence of any Samaritan temple on Gerizim remains controversial. Beginning in the mid-1980s, Y. Magen excavated in Tell er-Ras and the main peak of Gerizim and found no evidence of a temple there. Magen renewed the debate in the fall of 1995 when he claimed to have excavated the remains of the temple on Gerizim.[27] It is too early to say whether his identification will hold up. The Samaritan written sources are unnervingly silent regarding a temple. Only Abu'l Fath mentions that one existed that the Jews subsequently destroyed. On the other hand, an altar for sacrifices is mentioned in the *Tulidah,* and the Delos inscriptions contain a reference to the "temple [on] Argarizim." These witnesses appear to confirm Josephus's testimony regarding the existence of a Samaritan temple on Gerizim during the Hellenistic period. The widely varying interpretations of the available evidence suggest that resolution of this problem must await future archaeological discovery.

The significance of other data also remains uncertain. Coins found at Samaritan sites do not reflect the sect's peculiar concerns, and we should therefore speak of Samarian, not Samaritan, numismatics. There may be one important exception. Meyer Rosenberger has published 129 coins bearing images of Neapolis (now Nablus).[28] The majority of these pieces bear images of Mount Gerizim and of buildings erected on it. While some of the buildings cannot be identified, most scholars have assumed that the buildings are one or more temples. However, the temple may be one to Zeus and thus not Samaritan at all. The value of these coins for Samaritan studies may be chiefly to illustrate the dominant cultural symbols with which the ancient Samaritan community interacted.

Similarly, Josephus's account of the building of the temple in *Antiquities* seems suspect. It is parallel to the account of the building of the Jerusalem temple. Reinhard Pummer has commented: "The whole account of *Antiquities* 11:302–12 seems to be a midrash on Nehemiah 13:28."[29] Lester Grabbe earlier

---

[26] R. Bull, "Er-Ras," *EAEHL* 4 (1978): 1015–22.

[27] Yitzhak Magen's work has a popular summary in "Replica of Temple Found in Samaria," *BAR* 21.5 (September/October 1995): 24, 85, and his reports, "Mount Gerizim—a Temple City" and "First Phase of the Samaritan Temple on Mount Gerizim," appear (in Hebrew) in *Qad* 33.2 (2000), 74–118 and 119–24.

[28] Mayer Rosenberger, *Hippos-Sussita, Neapolis,* vol. 3 of *City Coins of Palestine: The Rosenberger Israel Collection* (Jerusalem: n.p., 1977).

[29] R. Pummer, review of Rita Egger, *Josephus Flavius und die Samaritaner: Eine terminologische Untersuchung zur Identitätsklärung der Samaritaner, JBL* 107 (1988): 771.

View of Mount Gerizim on a coin of Flavia Neapolis dating from the mid-second century to the early third century C.E. It portrays a large building on the left, presumably Hadrian's Zeus temple on Tell er-Ras, and another structure on the right, likely on the central peak since it is portrayed on a higher level and in appropriate perspective from Neapolis (Nablus). It is smaller and has been variously interpreted as a pagan sanctuary, an altar, and a Samaritan synagogue. *Courtesy of Reinhard Pummer, Biblical Archaeology* Review *and Zev Radovan, and the Israel Museum.*

suggested that the passage is a midrash on Nehemiah,[30] one that Josephus passes on rather than creates. Theodore H. Gaster said "that Josephus grotesquely patched his story together by fusing a Jewish and Samaritan tradition."[31] Josephus's account does seem to be more polemical than historical.[32]

Lack of monarchy eliminated much of the motivation for a temple, and the economic condition of postexilic Samaria would not have allowed temple building. Oppressed by Assyrians, Babylonians, and Persians, the Samaritans had minimal resources. The Jews did build a temple during the Persian period, apparently with some aid from the Persians (Ezra 1), but Haggai among others was less than impressed by the building.[33] A temple would require tremendous financial and labor resources that the evidence would suggest no Samaritan community ever had. Alan crown suggests in a forthcoming publication that the Samaritans (Samarians?) may have profited financially from the Persians in mid-fifth century B.C.E. intrigues.

---

[30] Lester Grabbe, "Josephus and the Judaean Restoration," *JBL* 106 (1987): 236–42.

[31] Theodore Gaster, "Samaritans," *IDB* 4 (1962): 192.

[32] Robert T. Anderson, "The Elusive Samaritan Temple," *BA* 54 (1991): 104–7.

[33] See Hag 2:3, "Who is left among you that saw this house in its ancient splendor? And how does it look to you now? Does it not seem to you like nothing at all?" See also Ezra 3:12.

Samaritan synagogues, on the other hand, appear at least as early as the first century.[34] The building of synagogues increased as the diaspora spread. Literary records describe far more synagogues than archaeological evidence can confirm, but several Samaritan synagogues have been uncovered in Israel and identified as such by inscriptions in mosaic floors decorating the buildings.[35] The inscriptions use the Samaritan script and in at least one instance (Sha'alvim) quote the sect's favorite texts (such as Exod 15:18). Six Samaritan inscriptions have come to light in Gaza and four in Emmaus. Presumably they served as lintels in either synagogues or private homes. One such stone, part of the Chamberlain-Warren collection, has been discussed in this volume. The size and quality of all the stones suggest that the engraved text was a public reminder of a cherished religious attitude or affiliation. Evidence of a Samaritan synagogue at Salbit is even more direct, though somewhat later (fourth century C.E.). There, a few miles west of Jerusalem, a mosaic floor and inscription have been found.

Aside from the inscriptional evidence from the buildings, there are no special architectural designs or features that identify a structure as a Samaritan synagogue. The Samaritan synagogues in the land of Israel all date between the fourth and the fifth centuries C.E. and are virtually of the same style as their Jewish contemporaries.

Baba Raba reportedly built a number of synagogues, some of which were renovations of structures ruined by the Romans. A decree to forbid Samaritan synagogues issued by the Roman emperor Commodus, son of Marcus Aurelius (ca. 192), is an early witness to their existence.

Samaritan documents name nearly a dozen synagogues within ten miles of Mount Gerizim, but inscriptions survive from only about half of them. Moving counterclockwise around the base of the mountain, one finds five sites to be of interest. Southeast of Gerizim is Kfar Qalil, where the existence of a synagogue is attested by the cryptogram in von Gall's Pentateuch manuscript G. An inscription found among the ruins of the village describes a synagogue that Abraham bar Emuna Avitara of the Gediah family built in 1214.

A short distance eastward at the present village of Rujeib is the site of a large synagogue, Kneshet Hapnina ("the Pearl"). Parts of this structure were reused in other area synagogues. For example, builders apparently removed as spoils columns from Kneshet Hapnina for use in the building of

---

[34] H. Kippenberg, *Garizim und Synagoge* (Berlin: de Gruyter, 1971), 158.

[35] Four synagogues can be identified as Samaritan with a great deal of confidence: Sha'alvim, Bet she'an, Ramat Aviv, and Huzn Ya'qub. For a careful discussion of Samaritan synagogues, see Reinhard Pummer, "Samaritan Synagogues and Jewish Synagogues," in *Jews, Christians, and Polytheists in the Ancient Synagogue* (ed. Steven Fine; New York: Routledge, 1999), 118–60.

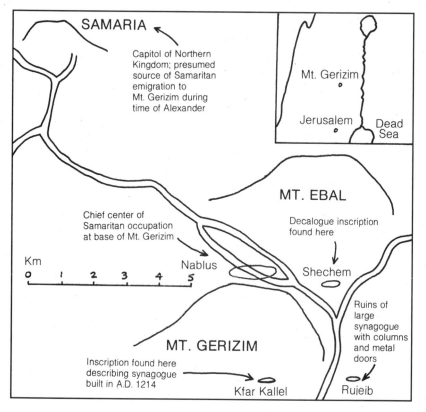

Samaritan synagogue sites near Mount Gerizim. *Courtesy of Robert T. Anderson.*

the synagogue at Shechem. A Decalogue inscription found there suggests that a synagogue existed in that city.

Evidence exists for several synagogues in Nablus. Chizn Jakub ("mourning of Jacob," for Joseph), located in the old market, inherited the metal doors of Kneshet Hapnina. Experiencing repeated destruction—by Zeno in 484, the Crusaders in the late Middle Ages, and later by the Mamluks—it eventually became a mosque. A Decalogue inscription (the one into which a crusader placed a cross) embedded in a wall supports Samaritan tradition attesting a prior synagogue on this spot built by Ikron ben Eleazar Muhoud in about 300.

In 1935 floods uncovered the remains of the other Nablus synagogue, notably a huge stone lintel bearing yet another Decalogue inscription, the Beit-el Ma inscription. A Samaritan family from Damascus refurbished an earlier synagogue on the site in the twelfth century during a period of tolerance under Saladin.

Samaritan synagogues also existed outside Palestine. The earliest is on the island of Delos, one of whose inscriptions implies that a man named Menippos underwrote its construction. A fourth-century C.E. ruin in Thessalonica was probably built by Siricus of Neapolis.[36] A letter of the Ostrogothic king Theodoric in the early sixth century refers to a Samaritan synagogue in Rome. By the late Middle Ages one existed in Cairo.

At least since Muslim times, Samaritan synagogues have been carpeted and without benches. As with most Samaritan religious practice, it is not clear whether the original precedent is native, Jewish, or Muslim, so integrally are the three faiths woven together.

---

[36] Alan D. Crown, "The Samaritan Diaspora to the End of the Byzantine Era," *AJBA* 2 (1974–1975): 107–21, esp. 115.

Chapter 10

The Chamberlain-Warren Collection

The Chamberlain-Warren collection at Michigan State University is the largest assemblage of Samaritan materials in the United States. The story of the collection's origin and rediscovery appears in Chapter 1. Our hope is that our work will help readers understand the importance of these materials and will also help keep the collection from sinking once again into obscurity. Future researchers will find there many stories that deserve telling.

As Chapter 1 recounts, the Samaritan collection was part of a much larger gift of materials donated to Michigan State University in 1950. For some time, the Samaritan manuscripts rested in three cardboard cartons stored under the east bleachers of the football stadium. The fascinating artifacts in this collection deserve fuller description, hence this final chapter.

THE INSCRIPTION

A white marble slab with dark blue veins measuring 31.0 x 12.2 x 5.0 cm was at the top of the first box reopened in the spring of 1968. It was Chamberlain-Warren 2472, described in Chapter 5 along with other relevant inscriptions. It contains the text of Exodus 15:3 and 11 in three lines within incised horizontal guidelines. Much of the face of the inscription bears a reddish stain. A cross section looked at from the end is trapezoidal in shape with the long side bearing the inscription. Only the ends and back remain unfinished, indicating that the top and bottom, as well as the inscription face were exposed. The back has been deeply scratched, and pieces of mortar still cling to it. The end on which the inscription begins carries the stump of what may have been a tenon to join the piece in place against the wall of a building. Slightly more than half of the inscription is missing.

Of course, the inscription begged to be read, identified, and placed in context. An inquiry to H. Neil Richardson at Boston University led to his colleague James Purvis, who was very much involved in Samaritan studies. The inscription then came to the attention of John Strugnell at Harvard University, who had published an article only months earlier on six

Samaritan inscriptions,[1] including this one that turned up in East Lansing. He knew about it because of a plaster casting made in Jerusalem a century before.

PENTATEUCHS

There were about sixty items in the three cardboard cartons. Apart from the inscription, three items stood out because of their size, leather pages, and apparent age. They were obviously Samaritan Pentateuchs, and the first task was to collate them against von Gall's work from early in the century.[2]

Three of the Chamberlain-Warren Pentateuchs date from the fifteenth century. One originated in Damascus and the other two in Egypt, apparently from the same scribe. The Damascene copyist was Seth Ahron b. Isaak b. Seth Ahron, who copied this text (CW 2473) in Damascus in 1470.[3] He was the scribe of at least one other Pentateuch (in 1481), designated C by von Gall,[4] which is currently in the collection of the Bibliothèque Nationale in Paris. He also witnessed a bill of sale in 1446–1447[5] and wrote another one in 1469.[6] His son was the scribe of Gothic C copied in 1504,[7] now owned by Westminster College in Cambridge, England.

Two other fifteenth-century Pentateuchs from the collection presumably come from the same scribe, though he used two different names, Aphiph and Ab Nishana. The genealogy of the two is the same: "son of Sedaqa son of Jakob son of Sedaqa son of Ab Chisda son of Obadiah of the family Munes." Three handwriting experts supervised by C. H. Romig of the School of Criminal Justice at Michigan State University examined both manuscripts. Two of them concluded that they were from the same hand. The third had some reservations, but generally agreed. "Both" scribes always indicated the date and how many manuscripts they had finished. There are eight manuscripts in various collections with one or the other of the names, and dates and order tally if both scribes are in fact the same person:

---

[1] Strugnell, "Quelques inscriptions samaritaines," 555–80.

[2] August von Gall, *Der Hebräische Pentateuch der Samaritaner* (Giessen: Töpelmann, 1914–1918). Von Gall compared and noted all the variant readings of forty complete manuscripts and about fifty fragments.

[3] It is cited in this work and further described in Robert Anderson, "Le Pentateuch samaritaine Chamberlain Warren CW 2473," *RB* 77 (1970): 68–75; and Itzhak Ben Zvi, "Migginzei Shomron," *Sinai* 13 (1943): 245–51, 308–18.

[4] Von Gall, *Hebräische Pentateuch,* iv.

[5] Von Gall, *Hebräische Pentateuch,* lxxiv.

[6] Von Gall, *Hebräische Pentateuch,* xxii.

[7] Von Gall, *Hebräische Pentateuch,* xxx.

1468–1469	Ab Nishana	(Sassoon 403/ Ben-Zvi כה)	Fifteenth
1474	Ab Nishana	(CW 2484/ Ben-Zvi לֹ)	Eighteenth
1476–1477	Aphiph	(von Gall I)	Nineteenth
1478	Ab Nishana	(Sassoon 404)	Twentieth
1481	Aphiph	(Ben-Zvi לֹד)	Twenty-eighth
1482	Ab Nishana	(von Gall Gothic R)	Twenty-ninth
1484	Aphiph	(CW 2478a)	Thirty-first
1485	Aphiph	(von Gall Gothic P)	Thirty-third

The 1474 and 1484 Pentateuchs are in the Chamberlain-Warren collection. Their author is thus a well-known figure in an important Egyptian family.[8] CW 2478a has the biblical text in both Samaritan Hebrew and Arabic.[9] It also contains two acrostics, four bills of sale, and a few colophons. CW 2484 contains two acrostics and three bills of sale.[10]

A fragment of another early manuscript was also found lodged between pages 147 and 148 of CW 2478a. At first it looked like a piece from CW 2484, but no part of that manuscript is missing. The fragment consists of thirteen lines on one side and twelve on the other, all from the book of Exodus. There are three reasons to suspect that it is from a manuscript predating the fourteenth century. First, it contains dots at the end of sentences, which later manuscripts do not bother to punctuate. Second, there are no indications of vocalization marks or columns of letters or words. Third, only a single letter is dragged to the left margin to justify it. Later manuscripts place two letters at the left margin. So far no other portions of this manuscript have come to light.

Three other Pentateuchs in the Chamberlain-Warren collection have special interest, although they are younger. Jacob b. Ahron b. Shelema wrote the first in Nablus. Its cover has a tooled arabesque design in red leather, making it the most attractive volume in the collection. It contains the Pentateuch in three languages, Samaritan Hebrew (completed in 1880), Aramaic (1893),[11] and Arabic (1894).

A note affixed to the page at which the volume was open in the Three Oaks Museum reads: "Pentateuch read 460 times by Jacob, Samaritan high priest." A series of notations in Arabic on the back flyleaf are

---

[8] Pummer, "Samaritans in Egypt," 223–24.

[9] The manuscript is cited in this work and further described in Anderson, "Le Pentateuch samaritaine," 550–63.

[10] It is cited in this work and further described in Anderson, "Le Pentateuch samaritaine," 368–80.

[11] The Samaritan Targum is a translation of the Samaritan Pentateuch into Aramaic during the third or fourth century C.E. Unlike the Jewish Targum, it lacks explanatory expansions.

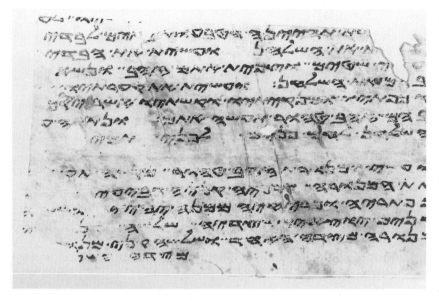

Manuscript fragment CW 2478b, containing Exodus 25:39–26:4.
Courtesy of Special Collections, Michigan State University Libraries.

Jacob's recordings of each of his readings, again 460. A letter from Barton to Chamberlain on November 30, 1920, claims the manuscript was purchased for £20.

The acrostic and colophons tell of difficult times. Eight of Jacob's ten children died in his lifetime, and three of them died while he was copying this volume:

> And I labored hard in the writing of this Torah from the year 1297 [Muslim dating = 1881] to the year 1311 [1894] from the opening of the wounds and strife and grief which came upon me from the death of my three children. And a change came upon me as in fasting I considered the distress which had come upon me in His name. I was motivated to proceed with this Torah and I was not able to contain my bitterness, but I did not stop when I finished it and went on to the Targum of the third Torah, making a division between Targum and Targum. I placed it upon the middle of this Torah.[12]

Jacob was born in 1841, married in 1859, and had ten children. He was high priest from 1861 until his death in 1916. Despite his personal poverty, he provided worthy leadership for the community. We are aware of an extensive literature that he produced as copyist, translator, and author. He was in contact with several influential people including William E. Barton, Moses

---

[12] From one of two notes at the end of the volume.

Gaster, and E. K. Warren. Gaster commissioned him to write several works and record a census of the Samaritan community at Nablus.[13]

A second modern (1912) volume of note is CW 2482, whose scribe was Ab Chisda, son of Jacob b. Ahron. As William Barton describes it, it is a "dainty little Pentateuch for which I see Mr. Warren paid the equivalent of $25.00 to help a crippled tailor. It was a high price, but is a very pretty little book."[14]

A note attached to the volume says that a tailor, Tahor son of Yaqob, bought a sewing machine with the money. The book is remarkable for its small size, measuring only 10.9 x 9.7 cm. Ten acrostics consisting of religious slogans are woven into the 489 pages of text. Two of them are laid out in circular form highlighting the words גריזים הר ("Mount Gerizim") by using selected letters in the text of Numbers 35:1–8. A colophon at the end of each of the biblical books tells what date the scribe finished copying the text.

A third Pentateuch (CW 10262) on paper is unique, both because it is in Arabic and because it presents several puzzles. Shelema the son of Jacob wrote it in 1685. The scribe copied from his model a number of personal notes about births, deaths, and the transfer of the manuscript. The same year witnessed the completion of another manuscript, probably a sister to this one. The second manuscript, in the Bibliothèque National in Paris, is designated "Arabe 3" and contains a note similar to that following Shelema's colophon at the end of Deuteronomy. The note in CW 10262 reads:

> This Holy Bible was copied from the old copy that was brought from Damascus from the house of its owner John the Damascene son of Qata. It was acquired and transferred to Paris by the Capuchin fathers in the year 1682.

This statement presents several puzzles. The note claims that the previous owner in Damascus was John son of Qata. Meanwhile, the note in Arabe 3 indicates that John (Yuhanna ibn Girgis ibn Qata of Damascus) was the scribe who finished it in Paris in 1685! Further, both Arabe 3 and CW 10262 agree that Capuchin priests brought the model from which they have copied to Paris. Who then was the Samaritan who was in Paris to copy Arabe 3 in the next year? Logically CW 10262 would also have been copied in Paris. How did it make its way back to Palestine and into the hands of Mr. Warren? And what happened to the model of both of these manuscripts? This mystery remains unsolved.

The Pentateuch manuscripts provide valuable historical evidence on many subjects. For example, there may be evidence of the identity of the first

---

[13] Robertson, *Catalogue*, 2:275–83.

[14] Letter from William Barton to F. W. Chamberlain dated November 30, 1920.

translator of the Samaritan Pentateuch into Arabic in a note in red ink at the end of the volume. Other Arabic translations reproduce it as well:[15]

> Said, the servant of God who humbly begs the forgiveness and blessings of his merciful creator, the son of Sa'ad al Basri, the Assyrian—may again the forgiveness of God be his. When I saw after reading the translation of the Holy Book with its unsound Arabic idiom which many claim was done by the venerable sheikh Abu Hassan the Syrian—may God have mercy on his soul—that this translation therefore could not be his. But it is the translation of the Jewish scholar al Fayoumi who truly erred in using the right Arabic idiom.

> For this major reason I have found it necessary to discharge my obligation toward serving a good cause by translating this Holy Book from the Hebrew and Syrian languages into a more correct Arabic text with the hope that more copies will be done by future scribes. This will also replace the erroneous copy of al Fayoumi. Hoping that by thus doing I will, by the help of God, secure for myself a good memory.

Several other paper volumes of pentateuchal books exist dating to the last three centuries, as do five paper scrolls of the Pentateuch. The latter are essentially identical and, although handprinted, seem to have been deliberately produced for sale to outsiders. Each is about 75 feet long and bears a seal of the high priest attesting its authenticity. A Three Oaks museum note dates one of them (CW 10322) to 1918. They all use paper bearing the letters "SSB" and crescent watermark (presumably a commercial trademark). There are no notes or acrostics.

THE SCROLL CASE

While reading the introduction to von Gall, Anderson noted a reference to a scroll case that E. K. Warren had purchased. Since no such item was in the three boxes that he had seen, Anderson called the museum, and the staff easily located it. As noted earlier, it is an impressive and attractive work, made of brass with inlaid silver design and bearing Samaritan inscriptions. It is 51 cm high, 19 cm in diameter. Abu'l Fath, son of Joseph, son of Jakob, son of Zophar of the Manasseh family crafted it in Damascus in 1524.[16]

---

[15] Haseeb Shehadeh, "The Arabic Translation of the Samaritan Pentateuch," in *The Samaritans* (ed. Alan Crown; Tübingen: Mohr, 1989), 489–516.

[16] It is described in this work and also in Hans Spoer, "The Description of the Case of the Roll of a Samaritan Pentateuch," *JAOS* 27 (1906): 105–7; and von Gall, *Hebräische Pentateuch*, lii.

The Chamberlain-Warren scroll case (CW 2465).
Photo by Robert T. Anderson.

Ironically, Anderson had seen the scroll case several years before in a University Museum exhibit, but it was displayed in a way that obscured its true nature. The exhibit focused on E. K. Warren, using items from various collections that illustrated his life. In one exhibit cabinet the scroll case lay open, so none of its decoration or inscription showed. In fact, its interior was not visible either because a twentieth-century paper scroll (probably CW 10322 listed above) had been partially unrolled and set into it. A tag beside it read:

In grateful appreciation for the thoughtfulness and understanding of Mr. Warren and his generous financial contributions, the Samaritans wished to express their thankfulness by presenting him with the original Pentateuch which, down through the centuries, still remained their cherished possession. The willingness of this people to place their most cherished religious possession in his hands was a sincere tribute to the deep feeling Mr. Warren held in his heart for the Samaritans. Their desire touched Mr. Warren and he told the Samaritans that he could not accept the Pentateuch, which was part of their heritage down through the centuries. Still wishing to present Mr. Warren with some tangible measure of appreciation, the Samaritans had a copy made by hand on parchment of the original Pentateuch as a gift to their benefactor and friend.

An undated, unsigned typewritten copy of this statement was recently found at the university. Another unsigned, undated, typewritten text describes the museum in Three Oaks and includes this sentence:

> In one of the cases there is a copy of the famous Samaritan Pentateuch, given to Mr. Warren by the high priest, in gratitude for the help he gave these people.

Von Gall speculates that this case may once have held the Abisha scroll in Nablus, but he does not lay out his evidence. German scholars did witness the transfer of the Abisha scroll in 1860 "from an old brass case,"[17] and it is possible that this container was the Chamberlain-Warren case.

LITURGIES

The six liturgical texts in the Chamberlain-Warren collection are among more than one hundred such manuscripts that appear in catalogues of Samaritan materials around the world. They cover the whole range of the sect's festivals, as well as rituals for special occasions like circumcision, marriage, and burial.

Most of these texts employ a cursive hand, although some responses and the featured letters of acrostics are in majuscule (capital) letters. Sections of Scripture are in continuous paragraph form or in small triangular patterns containing only the beginning of the verse and concluding with "etc." in Arabic. Hymns are usually written in two columns of doubled lines. Instructions to the congregation or leader usually occupy double lines of alternating ink color (red and black are favorites), and they contain many Arabic words and phrases. Catchwords, the first word of each left-hand page, usually appear at the bottom of the preceding right-hand page.

Hymns and poems of various length constitute a large part of the liturgy. The longer poems are usually acrostics, each stanza beginning with

---

[17] Barton, "War and the Samaritan Colony," 18.

a subsequent letter of the alphabet. Many are so well known that only the first few words appear in the book. Some are noted as a "Marqe" or a "Durran," indicating they are works of the theologian Marqe or his father, Amram Dare.

The liturgical works in the Chamberlain-Warren collection date from 1724 to 1904. The earliest work (CW 26343) represents parts of the *Defter* (the basic Samaritan prayer book) in Samaritan Hebrew with Arabic instructions, and it was copied by Murjan, son of Abraham, son of Ismail of the Danafite family. Four colophons mark the stages in the completion of the book. In 1860, Joseph, son of Israel, son of Ishmael, son of Abraham of the same family, made a copy of the liturgy for Sukkoth (CW 26344) in Samaritan with Arabic instructions. Later, another Danafite, Ishmael, son of Israeli, son of Ishmael, son of Abraham, wrote a copy of the Day of Atonement prayers (CW 10312) in the same languages. This text contains the curious phenomenon of almost a dozen poems by the same author spaced a hundred pages apart.

The remaining three Chamberlain-Warren liturgies are copies of Passover prayers with Arabic instructions. Salama, son of Amram, produced the first in 1888 (CW 2486). A unique feature of this text is the inclusion of a series of secular poems, all in Arabic and all exalting drinking wine, sailing, conversations, flowers, and maidens. In 1890 Ragib, son of Jakob, son of Ishmael, son of Abraham, copied CW 2480. In addition to the Passover prayers he drew many decorations including a diagram of the place of sacrifice on Mount Gerizim. Several acrostics identify the hymn writers. Chronologically, Barhum Sarawi is the last of the liturgical scribes, copying out CW 10323 in 1904.

MEMAR MARQE (TIBAT MARQE)

John MacDonald, who has edited and translated the *Memar Marqe,*[18] was aware of a half dozen manuscripts of the work. He posited two main types of fixed texts of *Marqe:* those copied by the Danafite family, and those written by the Levite family. The former is a superior text, more likely to follow the original reading. The copyist of the Chamberlain-Warren copy (CW 26349) was Ghazal ibn Isaak ibn Ibrahim ibn Isaak ibn Sadaqa ibn Ghazal. Of the three Levitical manuscripts that MacDonald could find, only one predated the Chamberlain-Warren text, and that was a very early copy from

---

[18] MacDonald, *Memar Marqah* and more recent work (in Hebrew) by Ben Hayyim, e.g., *Tibat Marqe: A Collection of Samaritan Midrashim* (Jerusalem: Israeli Academy of Sciences and Humanities, 1988).

1532. The other two dated to 1812 and 1870. In a colophon added to CW 26349 in 1835, Isaak, son of Salama, son of Ghazal, son of Isaak, son of Ibrahim, son of Ghazal, notes: "This book was read by the governor of Syria, Ibrahim Pasha, God make the people use this book." Ibrahim Pasha was governor of Syria from 1831 to 1840. It would be interesting to know the occasion of his meeting with the Samaritans.

Epilogue

It is never easy to preserve a tradition. The changing environment that gives it stability and uniqueness also works to destroy the practice of the tradition by robbing it of its significance and relegating it to the position of a quaint artifact of the past. Yet, the Samaritans, self-identified by their ability to keep a tradition, a religion, and a holy text, have stubbornly refused to disappear. The last chapter of their story has yet to be written. Having a history now spanning three millennia, the community has withstood the vicissitudes of history by keeping a firm grasp on a past stream of tradition. They are a vibrant community that gives no hint of soon passing from the stage of human drama.

This present volume is only a beginning. A host of unanswered questions about the history and culture of the Samaritan community remain. As has been shown, the Samaritans have been hounded by intrigue, occasional persecution, and frequent deception from the Hellenistic era right up through the modern era, and the ability of the community to survive through all this is not yet fully understood. It is truly remarkable that the community remains intact despite the domination of other cultural groups.

The Samaritan artifacts, in various collections around the world, are sure to provide clues to some of these mysteries of the past. The Chamberlain-Warren collection itself represents a fertile field of research not only for a fuller understanding of the Samaritan community but also for the wider discipline of biblical textual studies. The Samaritan Pentateuch, residing at the very heart of the Samaritan tradition, has yet to make its fullest contribution to the field of biblical studies. Textual studies in the Samaritan documents will occupy scholars for years to come.

One of the most fascinating and endearing aspects of the Samaritans is the ample humanness of the group. Never powerful, they have experienced all of the ups and downs common to every life. Perhaps it is their easy identification with the universal human experience that gives a certain fascination to this group of Keepers.

Bibliography

GENERAL WORKS

Anderson, Robert T. "Samaritans." Pages 940–47 in vol. 5 of *The Anchor Bible Dictionary*. Edited by D. N. Freedman. 6 vols. New York: Doubleday, 1992.

Bowman, John. *Samaritan Documents Relating to Their History, Religion, and Life*. Pittsburgh: Pickwick Press, 1977.

———. *The Samaritan Problem*. Translated by A. Johnson Jr. Pittsburgh: Pickwick Press, 1975.

Crown, Alan D. "New Light on the Interrelationships of Samaritan Chronicles from Some Manuscripts in the John Rylands University Library of Manchester." *Bulletin of the John Rylands University Library of Manchester* 55 (1972): 1–58.

Crown, Alan D., ed. *The Samaritans*. Tübingen: Mohr, 1989.

Crown, Alan D., and Lucy Davey, eds. *Essays in Honour of G.D. Sixdenier: New Samaritan Studies of the Société d'Études Samaritaines*. Sydney: University of Sydney Mandelbaum Publishing, 1995.

DeHaas, Jacob. *History of Palestine: The Last Two Thousand Years*. New York: Macmillan, 1934.

Gaster, Moses. *Studies and Texts in Folklore, Magic, Mediaeval Romance, Hebrew Apocrypha, and Samaritan Archaeology*. 3 vols. London: Maggs, 1925–1928. Repr., New York: KTAV, 1971.

Gaster, Theodore. "Samaritans." Page 192 in vol. 4 of *Interpreter's Dictionary of the Bible*. Edited by George Buttrick. 4 vols. Nashville: Abingdon, 1962.

Josephus. Translated by H. St. John Thackeray et al. 10 vols. Loeb Classical Library. Cambridge: Harvard University Press, 1926–1965.

Juynboll, Theodor G. J. *Chronicon Samaritanum cui titulus est Liber Josuae*. Leiden: Luchtmans, 1848.

MacDonald, John. *The Samaritan Chronicle No II (or Sepher Ha-Yamim) from Joshua to Nebuchadnezzar*. Beihefte zur Zeitschrift für die alttestamentliche Wissenschaft 107. Berlin: de Gruyter, 1969.

Montgomery, James A. *The Samaritans, the Earliest Jewish Sect.* Philadelphia: Winston, 1907. Repr., New York: KTAV 1968.

Pummer, Reinhard. *The Samaritans.* Leiden: Brill, 1987.

Purvis, James. "Studies on Samaritan Materials in the W. E. Barton Collection in the Boston University Library." Pages 134–43 in *Proceedings of the Fifth World Congress of Jewish Studies.* Jerusalem: World Union of Jewish Studies, 1972.

Robertson, Edward. *Catalogue of the Samaritan Manuscripts in the John Rylands Library.* 2 vols. Manchester: John Rylands Library, 1938, 1962.

Rothschild, Jean-Pierre, and Guy Dominque Sixdennier, eds. *Étude samaritaines Pentateuque et Targum, exégèse et philologie, chroniques.* Louvain-Paris: Peeters, 1988.

Sassoon, David Solomon. *Ohel David: A Descriptive Catalogue of the Hebrew and Samaritan Manuscripts in the Sassoon Library.* London: Sotheby, 1932; esp. 2:580–603.

Schur, Nathan. *History of the Samaritans.* Beiträge zur Erforschung des Alten Testaments und des antiken Judentums 18. New York: Lang, 1989.

Stenhouse, Paul. *The Kitab al Tarikh of Abu'l Fath.* Sydney: Mandelbaum Trust, 1985.

SAMARITAN ORIGINS

Astour, Michael C. "The Origins of the Samaritans: A Critical Examination of the Evidence." *Proceedings of the First International Symposium on Palestine Antiquities* 1 (1988): 9–53.

Boogaart, Thomas. *Reflections on Restoration: A Study of Prophecies in Micah and Isaiah about the Restoration of Northern Israel.* Groningen: Rijksuniveriteit te Groningen, 1981.

Brindle, Wayne A. "The Origin and History of the Samaritans." *Grace Theological Journal* 5 (1984): 47–75.

Cogan, Mordechai. "For We, Like You, Worship Your God: Three Biblical Portrayals of Samaritan Origins." *Vetus Testamentum* 38 (1988): 286–92.

Coggins, Richard J. *Samaritans and Jews: The Origins of Samaritanism Reconsidered.* Atlanta: John Knox, 1975.

———. "The Samaritans and the Northern Israelite Tradition." Pages 99–108 in *Proceedings of the First International Congress of the Société d'Études Samaritaines.* Edited by A. Tal et al. Tel Aviv: Chaim Rosenberg School for Jewish Studies, 1991.

Crown, Alan D. "Redating the Schism between the Judeans and the Samaritans." *Jewish Quarterly Review* 82 (1991): 17–50.

Egger, Rita. *Josephus Flavius und die Samaritaner: Eine terminologische Untersuchung zur Identitätsklärung der Samaritaner.* Freiburg, Switzerland: Universtätverlag, 1986.

Montgomery, James A. *I and II Kings.* International Critical Commentary. Edinburgh: T&T Clark, 1951.

Pummer, Reinhard. Review of Rita Egger, *Josephus Flavius und die Samaritaner: Eine terminologische Untersuchung zur Identitätsklärung der Samaritaner. Journal of Biblical Literature* 107 (1988): 771.

Purvis, James. *The Samaritan Pentateuch and the Origin of the Samaritan Sect.* Cambridge: Harvard University Press, 1968.

Rendsburg, Gary. *Linguistic Evidence for the Northern Origin of Selected Psalms.* Atlanta: Scholars Press, 1990.

Whaley, E. B. "Samaria and the Samaritans in the Josephan Corpus." Ph.D. diss., Emory University, 1989.

THE PERSIAN AND HELLENISTIC PERIODS

Bruneau, Philippe. "Les Israelites de Delos et la juiverie delienne." *Bulletin de correspondance hellénique* 106 (1982): 465–504.

Cohen, Shaye J. D. "Alexander the Great and Jaddus the High Priest according to Josephus." *Association for Jewish Studies Review* 7–8 (1982–1983): 41–68.

Collins, Adela Yarbro. "The Epic of Theodotus and the Hellenism of the Hasmoneans." *Harvard Theological Review* 73 (1980): 91–104.

Cross, Frank Moore. "The Discovery of the Samaria Papyri." *Biblical Archaeologist* 26 (1963): 110–21.

Fallon, F. "Theodotus." Pages 785–89 in vol. 2 of *The Old Testament Pseudepigrapha.* Edited by J. H. Charlesworth. 2 vols. New York: Doubleday, 1985.

Freudenthal, Jacob. *Alexander Polyhistor und die von ihm erhaltenen Reste judäischer und samaritanischer Geschichtswerke.* Vol. 1/2 of *Hellenistische Studien.* Breslau: Skutsch, 1874–1875.

Mor, Menahem. "The Persian, Hellenistic, and Hasmonaean Period." Pages 1–18 in *The Samaritans.* Edited by Alan D. Crown. Tübingen: Mohr, 1989.

Porten, Bezalel. *Archives from Elephantine.* Berkeley and Los Angeles: University of California, 1968.

Rappaport, U. "The Samaritans in the Hellenistic Period." Pages 281–88 in *New Samaritan Studies.* Edited by Alan D. Crown. Sydney: Mendelbaum Publishing, University of Sidney Press, 1995.

Rosenberger, Mayer. *Hippos-Sussita, Neapolis.* Vol. 3 of *City Coins of Palestine: The Rosenberger Israel Collection.* Jerusalem: n.p., 1977.

Rowley, Harold Henry. "Sanballat and the Samaritan Temple." *Bulletin of the John Rylands University Library of Manchester* 38 (1955): 166–268.

Schwartz, S. "John Hyrcanus I's destruction of the Gerizim Temple and Judaean-Samaritan Relations." *Jewish History* 7 (1993): 9–25.

Spiro, Abram. "Samaritans, Tobiads, and Judahites in Pseudo-Philo." *Proceedings of the American Academy for Jewish Research* 20 (1951): 279–355.

Stone, Michael, ed. *Jewish Writings of the Second Temple Period.* Philadelphia: Fortress, 1984.

Wacholder, Ben Zion. *Eupolemus: A Study of Judeo-Greek Literature.* Cincinnati: Hebrew Union College-Jewish Institute of America, 1974.

ROMAN PERIOD

Anderson, Robert T. "Samaritan Studies and Early Christianity." Pages 121–31 in *New Samaritan Studies.* Edited by Alan D. Crown. Sydney: Mendelbaum Publishing, University of Sidney Press, 1995.

Cohen, Shaye J. D. *Josephus in Galilee and Rome: His Vita and Development as a Historian.* Leiden: Brill, 1979.

Crossan, John Dominic. *The Historical Jesus.* San Francisco: Harper, 1992.

Dexinger, Ferdinand. "Limits of Tolerance in Judaism: The Samaritan Example." Pages 88–114 in *Jewish and Christian Self Definition.* Vol. 2 of *Aspects of Judaism in the Graeco-Roman Period.* Edited by E. P. Sanders. Philadelphia: Fortress, 1981.

Egger, Rita. "Josephus." Page 139 in *A Companion to Samaritan Studies.* Edited by Alan D. Crown, R. Pummer, and A. Tal. Tübingen: Mohr, 1993.

———. "Josephus Flavius and the Samaritans." Pages 109–14 in *Proceedings of the First International Congress of the Société d'Études Samaritaines.* Edited by A. Tal et. al. Tel Aviv: Chaim Rosenberg School for Jewish Studies, 1991.

Eusebius of Caesarea. *Chronicle.* Zurich: Weidmann, 1999.

Feldman, Louis H., and Gohei Hata, eds. *Josephus, Judaism, and Christianity.* Detroit: Wayne State University Press, 1987.

Fossum, Jarl. "Sects and Movements." Pages 293–389 in *The Samaritans.* Edited by Alan D. Crown. Tübingen: Mohr, 1989.

Grabbe, Lester. "Josephus and the Judaean Restoration." *Journal of Biblical Literature* 106 (1987): 236–42.

Hall, Bruce W. "From John Hyrcanus to Baba Rabbah." Pages 32–54 in *The Samaritans.* Edited by Alan D. Crown. Tübingen: Mohr, 1989.

————. *Samaritan Religion from John Hyrcanus to Baba Rabbah: A Critical Examination of the Relevant Material in Contemporary Christian Literature, the Writings of Josephus, and the Mishnah.* Sydney: Mandelbaum Trust, 1987.

Hammer, Heinrich. *Traktat vom Samaritanermessias: Studien zur Frage der Existenz und Abstammung Jesu.* Bonn: Carl Georgi, 1913.

Isser, Stanley Jerome. *The Dositheans: A Samaritan Sect in Late Antiquity.* Leiden: Brill, 1976.

Kasher, Aryeh. "Josephus on the Jewish-Samaritan Relations under Roman Rule (BCE 63–CE 70)." Pages 217–36 in *New Samaritan Studies.* Edited by Alan D. Crown. Sydney: Mandelbaum Publishing, University of Sidney Press, 1995.

Lowy, Simeon. *The Principles of Samaritan Biblical Exegesis.* Leiden: Brill, 1977.

MacDonald, John, and A. J. B Higgins. "The Beginnings of Christianity according to the Samaritans." *New Testament Studies* 18 (1972): 55–80.

Mare, W. Harold. "Acts 7: Jewish or Samaritan in Character?" *Westminster Theological Journal* 34 (1971): 1–21.

Munck, Johannes, ed. *The Acts of the Apostles.* Anchor Bible 31. Garden City, New York: Doubleday, 1967.

Richards, Earl. "Acts 7: An Investigation of the Samaritan Evidence." *Catholic Biblical Quarterly* 39 (1977): 190–208.

Scobie, Charles H. H. "The Origins and Development of Samaritan Christianity." *New Testament Studies* 19 (1973): 390–414.

Schneemelcher, Wilhelm, ed. *Writings Relating to the Apostles, Apocalypses and Related Subjects.* Vol. 2 of *New Testament Apocrypha.* Edited by Edgar Hennecke. Translated by R. McL. Wilson. Philadelphia: Westminster, 1965.

Strugnell, John. "Quelques inscriptions samaritaines." *Revue biblique* 74 (1967): 555–80.

Sylva, Dennis D. "The Meaning and Function of Acts 7:46–50." *Journal of Biblical Literature* 106 (1987): 261–75.

THE BYZANTINE PERIOD

Bowman, John, and Shemaryahu Talmon. "Samaritan Decalogue Inscriptions." *Bulletin of the John Rylands University Library of Manchester* 33 (1951): 211–36.

Crown, Alan D. "The Samaritan Diaspora to the End of the Byzantine Era." *Australian Journal of Biblical Archaeology* 2.3 (1974–1975): 107–23.

————. "Samaritan Religion in the Fourth Century A.D." *Nederlands theologisch tijdschrift* 41 (1986): 29–47.

————. "The Samaritans in the Byzantine Orbit." *Bulletin of the John Rylands University Library of Manchester* 69 (1986): 96–138.

Hamburger, Anit. "A Greco-Samaritan Amulet." *Israel Exploration Journal* 9 (1959): 43–45.

Kaplan, Jacob. "A Samaritan Amulet from Corinth." *Israel Exploration Journal* 30 (1980): 196–98.

Lagrange, Marie Joseph. "Inscription samaritaine d'Amwas." *Revue biblique* 2 (1893): 114–16.

Margain, Jean. "Une nouvelle amulette samaritaine portant le texte d'Exode 38:8." *Syria* 59 (1982): 117–20.

Meshorer, Ya'akov, and S. Qedar. *The Coinage of Samaria in the Fourth Century BCE.* Jerusalem: Numismatic Fine Arts International, 1991.

Pummer, Reinhard. "Inscriptions." Pages 190–94 in *The Samaritans.* Edited by Alan D. Crown. Tübingen: Mohr, 1989.

————. "Samaritan Amulets from the Roman-Byzantine Period." *Revue biblique* 74 (1987): 251–63.

Stenhouse, Paul. "Baba Raba." Pages 37–38 in *A Companion to Samaritan Studies.* Edited by Alan D. Crown, R. Pummer, and A. Tal. Tübingen: Mohr, 1993.

Taylor, W. R. "A New Samaritan Inscription." *Bulletin of the American Schools of Oriental Research* 81 (1941): 1–6.

ISLAMIC INVASION TO THE RENAISSANCE

Anon. "A Samaritan Torah Case." *Proceedings of the United States National Museum* 34 (1908): 708–44.

Crane, Oliver T. *The Samaritan Chronicle or the Book of Joshua.* New York: Alden, 1890.

Crown, Alan D. "The Abisha Scroll of the Samaritans." *Bulletin of the John Rylands University Library of Manchester* 58 (1975): 36–65.

————. "Some Traces of Heterodox Theology in the Samaritan Book of Joshua." *Bulletin of the John Rylands University Library of Manchester* 50 (1967): 178–98.

Gil, Moshe. *Palestine during the First Muslim Period (634–1099).* Tel Aviv: Tel Aviv University, 1983.

Giles, Terry. "The Chamberlain-Warren Samaritan Inscription CW 2472." *Journal of Biblical Literature* 114 (1995): 111–16.

Ibn Battuta. *Travels in Asia and Africa 1325–1354.* Translated by Hamilton A. R. Gibb. London: Routledge and Sons, 1929.

Kedar, Benjamin Z. "The Frankish Period." Pages 82–94 in *The Samaritans.* Edited by Alan D. Crown. Tübingen: Mohr, 1989.

Lewis, Bernard. "Egypt and Syria." Pages 175–230 in vol. 1 of *The Cambridge History of Islam.* Edited by P. M. Holt, A. K. S. Lambton, and B. Lewis. Cambridge: Cambridge University Press, 1970.

al-Makrizi, Taki-Eddin-Ahmed. *Histoire des sultans mamlouks de l'Égypte.* Translated by M. Quatremerie. Paris: Oriental Translation Fund, 1837.

Meyer, Martin A. *History of Gaza.* New York: Columbia University Press, 1907.

Poliak, Abraham N. *Feudalism in Egypt, Syria, Palestine, and the Lebanon, 1250–1900.* London: Royal Asiatic Society, 1939.

Pummer, Reinhard. "The Samaritans in Egypt." Pages 213–32 in *Études sémitiques et samaritaines offertes à Jean Margain.* Edited by Christian-Bernard Amphoux, Albert Frey, and Ursala Schattner-Rieser. Histoire du texte biblique 4. Lausanne: Éditions du Zèbre, 1998.

Shehade, Hasib. "When Did Arabic Replace the Samaritan Aramaic?" *A.B. Samaritan News* (October 15, 1978): 20–25.

Spuler, Bertold. *The Muslim World.* Vol. 2. Leiden: Brill, 1967.

Zertal, Adam. "The Samaritans in the District of Caesarea." *Ariel* 48 (1979): 115.

THE MODERN PERIOD

Barges, Jean Joseph L. "Les Samaritains de Naplouse: Épisode d'une pèlerinage dans les lieux saints." *Revue de l'Orient* 1 (1855): 1–81.

Barton, William E. "The War and the Samaritan Colony." *Bibliotheca sacra* 78 (1921): 1–22.

Crown, Alan D. "The Samaritans in 1984." *Yod* 11 (1985): 9–31.

de Sacy, Sylvestre. "Correspondance des Samaritains de Naplouse." Pages 1–230 in vol. 12 of *Notices et extraits des manuscrits de la bibliothèque du Roi.* Paris: 1831.

P. J. Bruns in Johann Gottfried Eichhorn. Pages 277ff. in vol. 13 of *Repertorium für biblische und morgenländische Literatur.* Leipzig, 1783.

Hamaker, H. *Aanmerkingen over de Samaritanen, en hunne Briefwisslung mit eenige Europesche Geleerden: Ter Gelegenheid von eenen nog onbekenden Samaritaanschen Brief.* In *Archief von Kerkelijke Geschiedenis* 5. Amsterdam, 1834.

Kautzsch, E. "Ein Brief des Hohenpriesters der Samaritaner Ja'kub ibn Harun." *Zeitschrift des deutschen Palästina-Vereins* 8 (1885).

Macalister, Robert Alexander Stewart. "Palestine: IV. From the Turkish Conquest to 1918." Pages 131–32 in vol. 17 of *Encyclopaedia Britannica.* Chicago: Encyclopaedia Britannica, 1953.

Simon, R. *Antiquitates ecclesiae orientalis.* London: George Wells, 1682.

Smith, T. R. *Huntintoni epistolae.* 1705.

della Valle, Pietro. *Viaggi.* Rome: Appresso Vitale Macarde, 1650–1663.

PENTATEUCH

Anderson, Robert T. "Clustering Samaritan Hebrew Pentateuchal Manuscripts." Pages 57–66 in *Étude samaritaines Pentateuque et Targum, exégèse et philologie, chroniques.* Edited by J. P. Rothschild and G. D. Sixdenier. Louvain-Paris: Peeters, 1988.

―――. "The Elusive Samaritan Temple." *Biblical Archaeologist* 54 (1991): 104–7.

―――. "Le Pentateuch samaritaine Chamberlain Warren CW 2473." *Revue biblique* 77 (1970): 68–75.

―――. "Le Pentateuch samaritaine Chamberlain Warren CW 2478a." *Revue biblique* 77 (1970): 550–63.

―――. "Le Pentateuch samaritaine Chamberlain Warren CW 2484." *Revue biblique* 74 (1972): 368–80.

―――. "Samaritan Pentateuch: General Account." Pages 390–96 of *The Samaritans.* Edited by Alan D. Crown. Tübingen: Mohr, 1989.

―――. "The Significance of Columned Letters and Words in Samaritan Manuscripts." *Proceedings of the Eastern Great Lakes and Midwest Society of Biblical Literature* 5 (1985): 21–27.

Barton, William E. "The Samaritan Pentateuch." *Bibliotheca sacra* 60 (1903): 5–42.

Beit-Arie, Malachi. *Hebrew Codicology.* Paris: Centre National de la Recherche Scientifique, 1976.

Ben Zvi, Itzhak. "Migginze Shomron." *Sinai* 9 (1941): 323–33.

―――. "Migginze Shomron." *Sinai* 10 (1942): 100–106.

―――. "Migginze Shomron." *Sinai* 11 (1942): 156–62.

―――. "Migginze Shomron." *Sinai* 12 (1943): 410–17.

―――. "Migginze Shomron." *Sinai* 13 (1943): 245–51, 308–18.

―――. "Migginze Shomron." *Sinai* 14 (1943): 17.

Crown, Alan D. "Samaritan Minuscule Paleography." *Bulletin of the John Rylands University Library of Manchester* 63 (1981): 330–68.

————. "Studies in Samaritan Scribal Practices and Manuscript History: I. Manuscript Prices and Values." *Bulletin of the John Rylands University Library of Manchester* 65 (1983): 72–94.

————. "Studies in Samaritan Scribal Practices and Manuscript History II: The Rate of Writing Samaritan Manuscripts and Scribal Output." *Bulletin of the John Rylands University Library of Manchester* 66 (1984): 72–94.

————. "Studies in Samaritan Scribal Practices and Manuscript History III: Columnar Writing and the Samaritan Massorah." *Bulletin of the John Rylands University Library of Manchester* 67 (1984): 349–81.

————. "Studies in Samaritan Scribal Practices and Manuscript History: IV. An Index of Scribes, Witnesses, Owners, and Others Mentioned in Samaritan Manuscripts, with a Key to the Principal Families Therein." *Bulletin of the John Rylands University Library of Manchester* 68 (1986): 317–72.

Gesenius, Wilhelm. *De pentateuchi samaritani origine, indole, et auctoritate commentatio philologico-critica.* Halle: Rengerian, 1815.

Goshen-Gottstein, Moshe. "The Textual Criticism of the Old Testament: Rise, Decline, Rebirth." *Journal of Biblical Literature* 102 (1983): 372–75.

Horgan, Maurya P. *Pesharim: Qumran Interpretations of Biblical Books.* Catholic Biblical Quarterly Monograph Series 8. Washington: Catholic Biblical Association of America, 1979.

Kahle, Paul. "Untersuchungen zur Geschichte des Pentateuch-textes." *Theologische Studien Kritiken* 88 (1915): 399–439.

Origen, *Hexapla.* Edited by Fridericus Field. Hildesheim: Olms, 1964.

Robertson, Edward. "Notes and Extracts from the Semitic Manuscripts in the John Rylands Library." *Bulletin of the John Rylands University Library of Manchester* 21 (1937): 244–72.

Sanderson, James. *An Exodus Scroll from Qumran: 4QpaleoExodm and the Samaritan Tradition.* Atlanta: Scholars Press, 1986.

Tal, Abraham. *The Samaritan Targum of the Pentateuch.* 3 vols. Tel Aviv: Tel Aviv University, 1980–1983.

Tigay, Jeffrey H. "An Empirical Basis for the Documentary Hypothesis." *Journal of Biblical Literature* 94 (1975): 327–42.

Tov, Emmanuel. "Pap. Giessen 13, 19, 22, 26: A Revision of the LXX?" *Revue biblique* 78 (1971): 355–83.

Von Gall, August Frh. *Der hebräische Pentateuch der Samaritaner.* Giessen: Töpelmann, 1914–1918. Repr., 1966.

Waltke, Bruce K. "Prolegomena to the Samaritan Pentateuch." Ph.D. diss., Harvard University, 1965.

————. "The Samaritan Pentateuch and the Text of the Old Testament." Pages 212–39 in *New Perspectives on the Old Testament.* Edited by J. Barton Payne. Waco, Texas: Word, 1970.

SAMARITAN RELIGION

Boid, Iain R. *Principles of Samaritan Halachah.* Leiden: Brill, 1989.

Bull, Robert. "Er-Ras." Pages 1015–22 in vol. 4 of *Encyclopedia of Archaeological Excavations in the Holy Land.* Edited by Michael Avi-Yonah and Ephraim Stern. 4 vols. Oxford: Oxford University Press, 1978.

Burrows, Miller. *What Mean These Stones?* New York: Meridian, 1957

Cowley, Arthur. E. *The Samaritan Liturgy.* Oxford: Oxford University Press, 1909.

Fossum, Jarl. *The Name of God and the Angel of the Lord.* Tübingen: Mohr, 1985.

Haran, Menahem. "The Song of the Precepts of Aaron ben Manir." *Proceedings of the Israel Academy of Sciences and Humanities* 5 (1974): 1–36.

Ben Hayyim, Ze'ev. *Tibat Marqe: A Collection of Samaritan Midrashim.* Jerusalem: Israel Academy of Sciences and Humanities, 1988 (Hebrew).

Kippenberg, Hans Gerhard. *Garizim und Synagoge.* Berlin: de Gruyter, 1971.

MacDonald, John. *Memar Marqah.* 2 vols. Berlin: Töpelmann, 1963.

————. *The Theology of the Samaritans.* London: SCM, 1964.

Magen, Yitzhak. "Mount Gerizim and the Samaritans." Pages 91–147 in *Early Christianity in Context, Monuments and Documents.* Edited by F. Manns and E. Alliata. Jerusalem: Franciscan Printing Press, 1993.

————. "First Phase of the Samaritan Temple on Mount Gerizim." *Qad* 33.2 (2000): 119–24 (Hebrew).

————. "Mount Gerizim—a Temple City." *Qad* 33.2 (2000): 74–118 (Hebrew).

————. "Replica of Temple Found in Samaria." *Biblical Archaeology Review* 21.5 (September/October 1995): 24.

————. "The Ritual Baths (Miqva'ot) at Qedumim and the Observance of Ritual Purity among the Samaritans." Pages 181–92 in *Early Christianity in Context, Monuments and Documents.* Edited by F. Manns and E. Alliata. Jerusalem: Franciscan Printing Press, 1993.

————. "Samaritan Synagogues." Pages 193–230 in *Early Christianity in Context, Monuments and Documents.* Edited by F. Manns and E. Alliata. Jerusalem: Franciscan Printing Press, 1993.

Pummer, Reinhard. *Samaritan Marriage Contracts and Deeds of Divorce.* 2 vols. Wiesbaden: Harrassowitz, 1993–1997.

————. "Samaritan Material Remains and Archaeology." Pages 135–77 in *The Samaritans.* Edited by Alan D. Crown. Tübingen: Mohr, 1989.

————. "Samaritan Synagogues and Jewish Synagogues." Pages 118–60 in *Jews, Christians, and Polytheists in the Ancient Synagogue.* Edited by Steven Fine. New York: Routledge, 1999.

————. *The Samaritans.* Leiden: Brill, 1987.

Reich, Ronny. "The Plan of the Samaritan Synagogue at Sha'valim." *Israel Exploration Journal* 44 (1994): 228–33.

Talmon, S. " 'Good Samaritan' a 'Good Israelite'." Pages 472–85 in *Wer ist wie du, HERR, unter den Gottern? Studien zur Theologie und Religionsgeschichte für Otto Kaiser zum 70 Geburtstag.* Edited by I. Kottsieper et al. Göttingen: Vandenhoeck & Ruprecht, 1994.

Thomson, J. E. H. *The Samaritans: Their Testimony to the Religion of Israel.* London: Oliver & Boyd, 1919.

Weiss, H. "The Sabbath among the Samaritans." *Journal for the Study of Judaism in the Persian, Hellenistic, and Roman Periods* 25 (1994): 252–73.

THE CHAMBERLAIN-WARREN COLLECTION

Anderson, Robert T. *Studies in Samaritan Manuscripts and Artifacts.* Cambridge: American Schools of Oriental Research, 1978.

Spoer, Hans. "The Description of the Case of the Roll of a Samaritan Pentateuch." *Journal of the American Oriental Society* 27 (1906): 105–7.

Index

N.B.: CW followed by a number is an item in the Chamberlain-Warren collection and can be found under that entry. Names in parentheses represent alternative spellings or names, or Samaritan family names.